# EVERYONE NEEDS A MENTOR

**Dr David Clutterbuck** is an international authority on mentoring and other 'helping to learn' behaviours. He and his team at Clutterbuck Associates work with companies around the world developing mentoring and coaching schemes. David co-founded the European Mentoring Centre, the primary resource for research and networking in mentoring within employment. He is an active mentor – his mentees range from chief executives to PhD students. He is visiting professor at Sheffield Hallam University and chairman of communication consultancy, the ITEM Group Ltd. He is author or co-author of more than 40 management books, including *Mentoring in Action*, *Mentoring Executives and Directors*, *Mentoring for Diversity* (forthcoming), *Techniques in Coaching and Mentoring* (forthcoming) and *Learning Alliances: Tapping into talent* (CIPD 1998). He can be contacted by e-mail at dclutterbuck@item.co.uk.

# Other titles in the series:

The Chartered Institute of Personnel and Development is the leading publisher of books and reports for personnel and training professionals, students, and for all those concerned with the effective management and development of people at work. For details of all our titles, please contact the Publishing Department:

*tel.* 020-8263 3387
*fax* 020-8263 3850
*e-mail* publish@cipd.co.uk

The catalogue of all CIPD titles can be viewed on the CIPD website:
www.cipd.co.uk/publications

# EVERYONE NEEDS A MENTOR

## Fostering talent at work

**Third edition**

**David Clutterbuck**

Chartered Institute of Personnel and Development

© David Clutterbuck 2001

First published 1985
Reprinted 1987 and 1990
Second edition 1991
Reprinted 1992, 1993, 1994, 1997, 1998, 1999

Design by Paperweight
Typeset by The Comp-Room, Aylesbury
Printed in Great Britain by
The Cromwell Press, Trowbridge


*British Library Cataloguing in Publication Data*
A catalogue record for this book is available from the
British Library

ISBN 0-85292-904-8

The views expressed in this book are the author's own, and
may not necessarily reflect those of the CIPD.

Chartered Institute of Personnel and Development,
CIPD House, Camp Road, London SW19 4UX
Tel: 020-8971 9000   Fax: 020-8263 3333
E-mail: cipd@cipd.co.uk
Website: www.cipd.co.uk
Incorporated by Royal Charter. Registered charity no. 1079797

# CONTENTS

# FOREWORD

When I wrote the first edition of *Everyone Needs a Mentor*, experience of formal, organised mentoring in Europe was limited to a handful of companies that had imported the concept from the USA to support graduates and high-flyers. Almost all the experience of mentoring, the development of theory and the academic research around the concept originated in the USA.

Sixteen years later, much has changed. The traditional US model of mentoring, described by Levinson, Kram and others, emphasises the use of the mentor's power, influence and authority on the mentee's behalf. The psychological contract is an exchange of practical help and guidance from the mentor for loyalty and respect from the mentee. Age and elevated position are key components.

It was this model that was reflected in the very first edition of this book. However, it soon became obvious that there was another very different model of mentoring that met the needs of European organisations and individuals much more closely. Developmental mentoring – which is now appearing in some US and Canadian organisations as well – emphasises helping the mentee become self-reliant and self-resourceful, being able to access multiple sources of support and learning. Here it is experience and wisdom that count more than age and position – while these sometimes go together, it is not universally true!

In Chapter 3 – a new addition to the book – we present a model that puts these two equally valid perspectives into context. This model is now the dominant means of explaining mentoring outside the USA.

This edition of *Everyone Needs a Mentor* draws on both models of mentoring, but its sympathies lie unashamedly with the European, developmental model. Hence the US term protégé, with all its overtones of unequal power and hands-on intervention by the mentor, is replaced by mentee, a more neutral (but still pretty horrible) term. The European Mentoring Centre has long offered a prize of a magnum of champagne for a term accepted as more appropriate by at least 50 per cent of the delegates at its annual conference – no sign yet of a viable alternative!!

The advice given in this book is based on my own and colleagues' experience of mentoring in hundreds of organisations around the world, in public, private and voluntary organisations; on our extensive research; and on the remarkably wide literature on mentoring that has emerged in the past two decades.

Much of this literature can be accessed through the European Mentoring Centre. However, it comes with a health warning – the vast majority of academic papers are of limited value and many are frankly misleading.

There are several reasons for this depressing statement. First, many studies fail to distinguish between very different types of relationship: for example, between the off-line role and the role of a direct supervisor; or between different styles and/or purposes of relationship. Much of the research suffers from inadequate definition of what is supposedly being measured. Very little research measures outcomes in other than broad generalisations.

Most US research uses Kathy Kram's insightful analysis of mentor functions (often confusingly using these as measures of outcomes as well). Unfortunately, while her basic division between career and psychosocial functions appears to be broadly valid, most of the subfunctions described are irrelevant or inimical to developmental mentoring. (This is perhaps not surprising, since Kram was measuring one variety of mentoring practice; the fault lies with academics unable or too lazy sufficiently to contextualise the relationships they were studying.)

For me, the past 15 years have been an exciting and rewarding journey working with academic colleagues such as Professor David Megginson of Sheffield Business School, and practitioners such as Jenny Sweeney and Kim Langridge, to build practical models and processes for developmental mentoring. Enhancing my own skills as a mentor has been one of the many side benefits. Along the way, we have developed standards for mentor competencies, explored the growing world of executive mentoring, helped establish good practice in mentoring for diversity and integrated mentoring into a wider portfolio of helping roles, including coaching and counselling.

Yet our current research programmes reveal that there is so much more to understand about these remarkably powerful developmental relationships – what makes them work, how to ensure that both parties find the experience rewarding, how to measure the quality or effectiveness of a mentoring relationship, and so on. If, in a further 16 years' time, I am still around to revise *Everyone Needs a Mentor* yet again, I am sure there will be much, much more to change in the light of experience and research over that time.

**David Clutterbuck**

# 1 MENTORING IN CONTEXT

Although mentoring is a concept that has only recently entered into the general vocabulary of business and society, it has a long pedigree. The word 'mentor' originally comes from Greek mythology. Odysseus, before setting out on an epic voyage, entrusted his son to the care and direction of his old and trusted friend Mentor. (In fact, Mentor was not particularly helpful. It was the goddess Athena who was young Telemachus's real mentor.) Yet in spite of the variety of definitions of mentoring (and the variety of names given to it, from coaching or counselling to sponsorship) all the experts and communicators appear to agree that modern mentoring has its origins in the concept of apprenticeship. In the days when the guilds ruled the commercial world, the road to the top in business began in an early apprenticeship to the master craftsman, a trader, or a ship's captain. This older, more experienced individual passed down his knowledge of how the task was done and how to operate in the commercial world.

Intimate personal relationships frequently developed between the master (or mentor) and the apprentice (or learner), especially as the apprentice acquired skills and began to substitute for his mentor. Marrying the master's daughter became an accepted means of providing career progression and retaining key skills with the firm.

The Industrial Revolution altered this emphasis, demanding large numbers of recruits, which swamped personalised attention. Apprenticeship often degenerated to the stage where it involved depersonalised mass training in technical areas. Within the large corporation there grew up informal, often hidden, methods of passing on the experience of old-timers to young recruits. At the lower levels, a supervisor might 'keep an eye on' a promising employee. Senior managers might identify a potential high-flyer and provide him or her with confidential advice and encouragement. Therefore, although the term may not have had currency, mentoring was nonetheless at work.

In recent years, mentoring has also spread beyond the world of careers and work to embrace a wide spectrum of community needs. In the UK, for example, there are active mentoring programmes to help disadvantaged schoolchildren and university students to stick at and concentrate on their studies, young offenders to change their lives, teenage mothers to cope with their multiple responsibilities, head teachers to improve the management of their schools, and programmes to help the unemployed of all ages into the workforce. There are also schemes to encourage creativity in the Arts and Sciences, and to support owner-entrepreneurs in developing their own competence in line with the increasing demands of their businesses.

There is, however, considerable confusion over what mentoring is and is not. To some, it is synonymous with coaching (itself a word given different, often contradictory meanings). To others, it is a form of advice-giving, close to consulting. To others, it is akin to counselling, although not necessarily at the therapeutic end of the counselling spectrum. In the next chapter, we try to reconcile some of these differences in view.

It doesn't help that there are at least two very different schools of thought about the nature and purpose of mentoring, which can be broadly described as the US and the European, or sponsoring and developmental. The US or sponsoring school originates with Ralph M. Stodgill, who referred to the mentor in the late 1960s as 'an ambitious authority figure'. Daniel Levinson (1978), 10 years later in a study of 40 mentoring relationships, described him as 'a mixture of parent and peer. His primary function is to be a transitional figure in a man's development'. He calls mentoring 'one of the most complex and developmentally important relationships a man can have in early adulthood'. Other communicators refer to the mentor as 'a role model . . . a guide, a tutor, a coach and a confidant'. In the words of Agnes Missirian (1982), Professor of Management at Bentley College in Waltham, Massachusetts, 'there is a very strong emotional bond and, according to research, personal identification with the mentor as distinct from a sponsor' (ie the mentor is both a sponsor and a friend/guide).

## Definitions

Dr Audrey Collin (1979), of the School of Management at Leicester Polytechnic, gathered a number of largely US definitions of mentoring for an article in *Industrial and Commercial Training* magazine. Mentors were said, for example, to be 'influential people who significantly help you reach your major life goals'. Mentoring is 'a process in which one person [mentor] is responsible for overseeing the career and development of another person [mentee] outside the normal manager/subordinate relationship'. Alternatively, mentoring is 'a protected relationship in which learning and experimentation can occur, potential skills can be developed, and in which results can be measured in terms of competencies gained rather than curricular territory covered'.

Words like 'oversee' and 'responsible for' project an image of a hands-on kind of relationship with a clear sense of senior and subordinate. The word 'protégé' also carries distinct overtones of applied power. These concepts are carried on into most of the North American and some European academic literature on mentoring, and in particular, in how mentoring success is measured. It is worth at this point making the controversial but in my view accurate point that *the vast majority of US literature on mentoring is of minimal value in planning and understanding mentoring in a European context*, because it begins from fundamentally different assumptions about the role and nature of mentoring.

Mentoring schemes in the UK and Europe, and to a large extent in Australia/New Zealand, tend to conform to the official definition of the European Mentoring Centre: mentoring is 'off-line help by one person to another in making significant transitions in knowledge, work or thinking'. The rationale behind this is as follows:

☐ *Off-line* is appropriate because it is difficult to be fully open in a relationship where one person has authority over the other. In the few cases where mentoring relationships have been set up between individuals and their managers, the managers in particular have found a conflict of role – either the mentee holds back information, or the managers find themselves in possession of confidences, which they cannot use without damaging the relationship. There are rare occasions when an off-line mentoring relationship becomes an in-line relationship, and, if it is sufficiently strong, may continue informally. However, most schemes would withdraw support for a formal mentoring relationship in these circumstances.

☐ *Help* is a weak term, but it covers a wide range of resources for which the mentee can turn to the mentor – from direct advice, to simply listening. A key skill for the effective mentor is to be able to adapt the nature of the help given to the mentee's needs at the time.

☐ *One person to another:* In developmental mentoring, the hierarchy is not important – it is the experience gap that matters. Peer mentoring is increasingly common, as is upward mentoring, where the mentor is more junior in terms of the hierarchy. Top management at GE all have young e-literate mentors who keep them abreast of new technology. Two short cases at the end of this chapter illustrate upward mentoring in more detail.

☐ *Significant transitions:* Mentoring schemes and mentoring relationships need some sense of purpose if they are to achieve benefits for the participants. We will explore some of this in Chapters 7 and 8. One of the most common problems with formal mentoring schemes is that mentor and mentee meet, each hoping the other will define what they should be talking about. This is not a recipe for success!

Another useful definition within the developmental mentoring context is by Eric Parsloe (1992):

> To help and support people to manage their own learning in order to maximise their potential, develop their skills, improve their performance, and become the person they want to be.

A relatively concise description of the essentials of a developmental mentoring relationship comes from a website designed by my colleague Jenny Sweeney as follows:

> Mentoring is a partnership between two people built upon trust. It is a process in which the mentor offers ongoing support and development opportunities to the mentee. Addressing issues and blockages identified by the mentee, the mentor offers guidance,

counselling and support in the form of pragmatic and objective assistance. Both share a common purpose of developing a strong two-way learning relationship.

Mentoring helps mentees and mentors progress their personal and professional growth. Its primary focus tends to be on the acquisition of people skills which enable individuals to operate effectively at high levels of management. The aim of mentoring is to build the capability of the mentees to the point of self-reliance while accelerating the communication of ideas across the organisation.

The mentoring relationship is confidential. The mentor offers a safe environment to the mentee within which they can discuss work-related issues and explore solutions to challenges. For this reason, in a formal mentoring scheme, mentors are rarely in a line relationship; they are off-line. In this way, the mentors are not required to evaluate the current work performance of the mentees. They are there to help the learner manage his or her own learning.

Mentors can help individuals reach significant decisions about complex issues. Through skilful questioning, they help clarify the mentee's perspective while bringing an additional view to bear on the issues. Mentors are not there to solve problems but rather to illuminate the issues and to help plan ways through them.

Mentoring is a positive developmental activity. Mentors can discuss current issues relating to the mentee's work, offering insights into the ways the organisation works, how the informal networks operate and how they think about the challenges and opportunities they encounter.

Mentors can advise on development and how to manage a career plan; they can challenge assumptions; and, where relevant, they can share their own experience. Mentoring has proved to be very effective in transferring tacit knowledge within an organisation, highlighting how effective people think, take decisions and approach complex issues.

Sharing views and ideas builds understanding and trust. The mentor and mentee relationship often evolves into a key friendship, invaluable when difficult decisions arise.

## Qualifications and standards

The confusion about what mentoring is and what it aims to achieve has spilled over into the world of standards and qualifications, particularly in the UK. A number of organisations representing specific interest groups have attempted to 'capture' mentoring, whether or not what they do falls into the mainstream definitions. Other organisations have developed standards or even National Vocational Qualifications, based on very specific, very narrow applications of mentoring, or have designated their coaching qualifications as mentoring (presumably to make them sound more upmarket!).

Many practitioners with long experience in mentoring regard this trend with alarm, not because they wish to impose a particular view but because this kind of fractionation undermines the essential *inclusivity* of mentoring. The generic standards developed by the University of North London in collaboration with Herts TEC, Harrow Business School, University of Westminster, the Oxford School of Coaching and Mentoring and the European Mentoring Centre go a long way to reinforcing that sense of inclusivity and encouraging people to view mentoring as a broad range of approaches to helping others grow. Organisations wishing to develop their mentoring programmes alongside a set of standards should be very critical of what is on offer, to ensure that it really does meet the purposes of their scheme.

## How mentoring has developed over recent decades

The innovation that initiated the explosion of mentoring applications over the past three decades was the formalisation of the process. Rather than simply let mentoring happen, companies in the USA decided to give it a helping hand, providing a structure that allowed the organisation to ensure that potential high-flyers always had a more senior figure to guide them and 'oversee their careers'. Over time, the benefits of mentoring were extended to other groups of employees, with a view to redressing some of the inequalities in opportunity in employment, and gradually the concept spilled over into companies' relationships with schools and the community, and then into a wide variety of volunteering activities, independent of the business world. In the UK, where a similar series of transitions has occurred, at least one government department has apparently been working on the wildly erroneous assumption that mentoring is simply an aspect of volunteering, which happens to have been borrowed by companies for their internal purposes. This is one of many strong indications of the failure to integrate good practice and experience between the sectors – even in companies that have internal mentoring programmes and community mentoring schemes, there is often little or no benchmarking between them. In the next chapter, we explore the recent history of mentoring in more depth.

## UPWARD MENTORING: THE CABINET OFFICE AND PROCTER & GAMBLE

### The Cabinet Office

This case was first published in *Mentoring in Action* (Clutterbuck and Megginson 1999). Leslie Martinson was at the time a civil servant in the Cabinet Office, with a role that demanded she obtain a good instinctive understanding of the world of training. As this was not her core background, Leslie enrolled on a two-year advanced diploma programme for trainers, which encouraged participants to seek mentors. The mentor she chose was someone younger and in a grade below, but with very extensive training experience. Ignoring the status difference made for relaxed, often humorous but intense meetings, where Leslie was able to explore her progress towards becoming an effective trainer, plus a number of other personal development goals she had set for herself. The relationship survived changes of jobs on both sides, including one that took Leslie into the position of supervising her mentor's boss. The relationship dissolved as she completed the programme and both of them moved on to new fields.

### Procter & Gamble

A higher turnover amongst women in junior and middle management posts was one of the key triggers for the Mentoring Up programme introduced in P&G's marketing division a while ago. The traditional response to this kind of problem in mentoring terms is to institute a glass ceiling programme, under which senior executives (usually predominantly male) would adopt younger, more junior protégés and nurture their progress. In this case, however, the company was astute enough to recognise that this approach (which was considered) would simply reinforce the cultural aspects of the problem. These could only be addressed by creating an environment in which the male executives learned to understand the problems of diversity for themselves.

The programme that resulted provided male managers with female mentors, usually more junior than themselves, whose role was to:

☐ provide them with informal, non-threatening feedback on how to manage issues specific to women

☐ act as a sounding-board.

At the same time, the programme allowed the women mentors to develop quality relationships with people at senior level and hence to become more visible within the organisation.

The results of the initiative include a remarkable improvement in the retention problem.

# 2 MENTORING IN THE PAST TWO DECADES

The USA, where mentoring first became a serious issue for management discussion and study, continues to have a large number of programmes. Some organisations have discontinued programmes, however – the result, it appears, of overenthusiastic, poorly managed schemes that failed to achieve their potential.

In the UK, though, the pace of growth of mentoring increased from the mid- to late 1980s and continued to increase through the 1990s. An Industrial Society Best Practice survey in 1995 found that mentoring was used to some extent by slightly less than half of companies, with larger companies more likely to have schemes. Schemes were more prevalent in financial services and utilities than in manufacturing and services, and tended to be for relatively small number of employees.

There have been few extensive studies of mentoring activity since that date, although at least one international study of good practice in mentoring scheme management is in progress at the time of writing. A reasonable current picture of the extent of mentoring activity – based on field experience and conference discussions – is as follows:

☐ Most sizeable organisations have some experience of mentoring.

☐ In most cases, this consists of small pilot programmes for specific target groups, or the provision of external mentors for executives.

☐ Many companies, particularly in the UK, participate in community mentoring schemes (where employees volunteer to mentor young people in school, for example); however, there is rarely a link between this activity and mentoring within the organisation.

☐ In most cases, mentoring is not integrated with other developmental initiatives.

A 1987 study of mentoring in eight countries – Australia, France, Germany, Holland, Eire, Spain, the USA and the UK – found that a third of schemes were pilots (up to 40 per cent in some countries). Just under half of all schemes had been running for two years or less. One scheme in five had been in operation for 10 years or more.

Neither of these now dated studies benchmarked the respondents to check whether they had a common understanding of what mentoring involved, nor whether they had a structured approach. There is a high probability that some respondents did not distinguish clearly between coaching and mentoring. Moreover, mentoring activity in one division or subsidiary of a large and complex organisation is not evidence of a commitment to a mentoring culture.

In short, it is still very difficult to estimate the real level of mentoring activity in organisations. That there has been year-on-year increase is generally accepted, but there is no confirmatory evidence beyond the anecdotal.

Among key conclusions of the survey were:

☐ Most schemes were used to 'develop young professionals'.
☐ British and Australian companies were most receptive to the concept of a formal mentoring programme. Even at this stage, many US companies were tending more towards the informal approach.
☐ Few schemes had been discontinued and 93 per cent of companies expected their schemes to carry on. Where mentoring had failed, the main reason was inadequate training for the mentors.
☐ The main impediments to a successful scheme were reported as 'time commitment for mentors, company culture and resistance from top management'.

By the new millennium, the emphasis of mentoring had spread to encompass a much wider spectrum of situations. While graduate entry schemes remain significant, they have been joined by extensive schemes aimed at tackling diversity issues, an explosion of mentoring for executives at the top of organisations, programmes aimed at helping women to return to work, or to settle in when they have done so, and even programmes, such as that conducted by Nestlé in Scandinavia, to help people make the transition into retirement. In addition, there are companies, such as engineers Brown and Root and many of the international finance houses, which aspire to giving everyone the opportunity to have a mentor.

## The scope of mentoring

Some examples of recent initiatives include:

☐ Ericsson, the Swedish mobile telephone company, uses a global mentoring programme aimed at international high-flyers, helping them to become comfortable in a global culture.

☐ BOOST is an innovative project in Zimbabwe to help the brightest, most entrepreneurial graduates set up their own businesses, which will in turn hire other graduates. Against a background of political turmoil and very high unemployment amongst graduates, the scheme has received considerable backing at home and abroad. The mentors are all successful businesspeople from the local economy.

☐ British Aerospace, which recruits some 400 graduates annually, aims to give each of them a mentor for at least the first year.

☐ The Cabinet Office manages a programme for unleashing the potential of people with severe disability. It pairs the disabled person with a more senior civil servant, who can help him or her think constructively about issues of career management and personal development.

☐ A major London solicitor's practice uses mentoring to help people make the transition to partner. What it takes to be considered partner material is so difficult to explain or demonstrate that formal training doesn't really help. Mentoring provides a useful way of passing on this largely intuitive understanding.

☐ For Shell in Brunei and elsewhere, a major challenge is how to speed up the development of local nationals to take over from the expatriate engineers and managers. Mentoring provides a practical and culturally acceptable route to making this happen.

- The World Bank attracts the best and brightest people from around the world, making it a hothouse of ideas and potential cultural conflict. From a handful of relationships two years ago, mentoring has spread to some 2,000 pairs, in a variety of schemes, each either providing a support network for a particular ethnic or functional group, or building bridges between them.

At a community level, we have seen programmes that address various issues:

- Birmingham's BEAT scheme, which addresses the special needs of young people leaving prison, placed most of its youngsters into work and kept them out of court. In addition, some of the mentors were long-term unemployed people who gained so much self-confidence helping the young offenders into employment that they, too, returned to full-time work.
- FAS, the Irish Ministry of Employment, is helping thousands of difficult-to-employ young people – many of them from families with no history of stable employment for generations – to acquire self-confidence and skills with a combination of FAS-delivered training, coaching from colleagues in their work placement and mentoring from a senior manager in the placement company.
- Mentors help musically talented young people stick to it through the difficult teenage years when other attractions tug at their attention.
- There are now a number of programmes where volunteers from local companies or from the community in general spend time helping children with poor literacy and numeracy skills catch up. (There is some debate about whether this is really mentoring, even where there is an additional role of helping the young person think about life goals, but we'll avoid that for now.)
- Black students at risk of dropping out of university have a mentor for the first year to help them settle in.
- Some schools now provide each newcomer with a peer mentor from two years above to help them settle in. The arrangement also helps build the self-respect and maturity of the young mentor. Another group increasingly targeted

within schools as potential mentees is children at risk from bullying.

The list could go on and on. Suffice to say that any occupation from theatre management to farm work is likely to harbour formal or informal mentoring arrangements, as is any area of education or learning.

## Room for failure

Not all programmes are a success, however. One large UK retailing company initiated a campaign to create mentors in every one of its branches. However, it provided little or no central support for this initiative and such mentoring as happened two years later was spasmodic, informal and unrewarded. Most staff did not even know the programme existed.

Such failures in support are commonplace, unfortunately. One company in an Industrial Society/ITEM benchmark survey (1990) had introduced a scheme then promptly changed the organisational structure, putting so much pressure for operational results on the mentors that they had no time to spare for building the relationship with their mentees. The scheme did not even get off the ground and the company switched its attention to a new fad, interactive video, with much the same inadequate level of preparation.

The Industrial Society/ITEM survey found that relatively few companies with mentoring schemes gave mentors formal training, although more than half offered some form of support, mostly through workshops and regular meetings of mentors to exchange views and discuss problems. The 1995 Industrial Society found that while nearly half of companies offered mentors guidance notes, only 37 per cent provided training in mentoring concepts and 31 per cent in coaching and counselling skills. Worse still, only 14 per cent offered training to mentees; 24 per cent relied on the mentor to explain to the mentee what was expected. The picture that emerges, therefore, is one of growing enthusiasm, but frequently without the support or scope that schemes need to be a real success or to influence the business.

The USA has already encountered the problems that result from such failures. In a seminal article entitled, 'Take my mentor, please', management journalist Peter Kizilos (1990) reports: 'The value of the ancient master-apprentice relationship had been recognised by post-industrial theoreticians. The secret to success wasn't found in some new-fangled seminar. Advancement depended on finding a high-muck-a-muck who would adopt you like a son or daughter.'

In practice, however, he says, high expectations by mentees (victims of hype by both the business media and overenthusiastic researchers and consultants) have been compounded by corporations that undervalue personal and professional development, and which often see formal mentoring programmes as a quick fix. He quotes Michael Zey (1984), a veteran writer on mentoring: 'Managers will say, "Let's draft a few people to be in the program. Let's line them up and bring in a speaker to talk about mentoring." Then they go off and leave the mentors and mentees on their own.'

Current opinion on mentoring in the USA appears to be polarising between the 'traditionalists', who have made a success of formal programmes through thorough preparation and strong involvement of both line managers and the training department, and the proponents of informal mentoring. The latter agree that 'true mentor-mentee relationships are rare. They must develop naturally, not at gun-point.' Field experience provides a wealth of supporting anecdotes. In one company, where managers were given two mentors – one they selected themselves and one assigned to them – the latter relationships were seen as more uncomfortable, less trusting and less useful. Forced coupling can fuel discontent, anger, resentment and suspicion. The critics argue that a more effective approach is for people to establish a *network of mentors* – a conclusion supported by a 1984 survey of 7,000 managers at Honeywell Inc in Minneapolis.

In the UK, a number of organisations are following similar reasoning. A large educational institution, for example, recognising that there will be little direct support from the top for a formal, highly structured mentoring programme, assessed instead an informal scheme in which mentors were trained and sent in search of suitable mentees. A financial services company included mentoring as a core skill in its development programme for *all* managers. Mentor-mentee relationships are brought about by suggestions from the training department, from line managers or at the request of would-be mentees.

We will return to the theme of formal v informal in Chapter 4. For the moment, however, suffice to say that the evidence on the ground suggests strongly that the programmes that deliver best results are those that have both commitment from the top and a broad framework or structure under which mentoring relationships can develop with the degree of support they need. The case of District Audit, which audits public-sector organisations, illustrates the point. The informal mentoring that was taking place was too little, too unfocused and was not crossing the organisational barriers, such as the head office/field divide. On launching a formal mentoring programme, concerned that the heavy task orientation of the business would make it very difficult for people to spend quality time in developmental discussions, the CEO David Prince made a point of visiting every training session for mentors or mentees, or deputising another board member to do so. Prince himself spoke eloquently about his own mentoring relationship and how it helped him. A year or so later, when some 50 relationships were under way, virtually all reported significant learning taking place – for both mentor and mentee. In addition, there was a measurable improvement in the quality and quantity of interpersonal communication between head office and the field.

## Summary

Mentoring has undergone rapid evolution in recent years and is likely to continue to do so. It is hoped that the coming decade will see increased cross-fertilisation between different styles and application of mentoring, particularly across the business, education and community sectors.

# 3 MODELS OF MENTORING

Understanding the dynamics of mentoring relationships isn't necessarily straightforward, as Figure 1 indicates. Every relationship operates within a *context*, which for formal mentoring involves the culture and/or climate of the organisation, the structure and purpose of the scheme, and the background of the mentor and mentee. Each mentoring pair brings to the relationship a set of *expectations* about the purpose of the relationship, about their role and the behaviours they should adopt, and about the likely outcomes. Many or all of these expectations will be influenced by the context. The interaction between the mentor and mentee is a self-reinforcing system – each party's *behaviour* will influence the behaviour of the other. This in turn will influence the *process*, eg how frequently they meet, how deeply they explore issues. And finally, the effectiveness of the process will have a strong influence on the *outcomes*, which can be categorised as either supporting (often referred to in the literature as psychosocial) or career-oriented. Outcomes will normally need to be positive for both sides, in order for the relationship to continue much beyond the short term – if either mentors or mentees feel they are getting nothing for their efforts, the relationship will falter and die.

The challenge is to provide ways of describing what we mean by mentoring that are both academically sound and simple for people to understand and apply. In this chapter, we explore a basic model that fits those criteria, then some alternative perspectives on mentoring that help to distinguish it from other forms of helping others to learn and grow.

## The two dimensions of 'helping to learn'

The core model of mentoring – the dynamic that drives a high proportion of the schemes and programmes around the world outside the USA – derives from two key relationship variables.

## *Figure 1* THE CONTEXT OF MENTORING

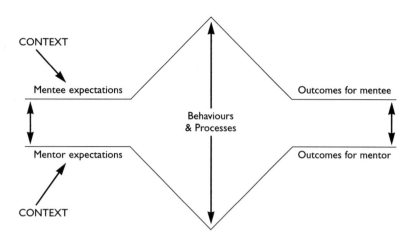

The first of these is 'Who's in charge?' If the mentor takes primary responsibility for managing the relationship (by deciding the content, timing and direction of discussion, by pointing the mentee towards specific career or personal goals, or by giving strong advice and suggestions), then the relationship is directive in tone. If he or she, by contrast, encourages the mentee to set the agenda and initiate meetings, encourages the mentee to come to his or her own conclusions about the way forward and generally stimulates the development of self-reliance, then the relationship is relatively non-directive (see Figure 2).

Support for this dimension of helping behaviour comes from a variety of resources both within the mentoring literature and in the parallel literatures on counselling and coaching as well as interviews and appraisal. For example, Barham and Conway's (1998) study of the influence of cultural factors on mentor behaviour concludes that, where managers expect their normal role to be that of expert, 'The style of the mentoring relationship will be more didactic and less empowered from the mentee's perspective.' Where the culture expects managers to be facilitators, however, 'The balance of the relationship will be more equal and it will be about mutual learning and sharing. There will be an empowered "feel" to the mentoring relationships.'

Recent studies suggest strongly that the most effective relationships – where personal development is the desired outcome

– are those in which the mentee is relatively proactive and the mentor relatively passive or reactive. The opposite is probably true for relationships that are more focused on sponsorship behaviours.

*Figure 2* **TWO DIMENSIONS OF HELPING**

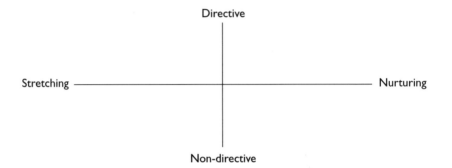

The second dimension relates to the individual's need. Is it primarily about learning – being challenged and stretched – or about nurturing – being supported and encouraged? Again, this is a dimension well established in the general psychological literature, and in particular that on leadership.

Blake and Mouton (1964), Schriesheim and Murphy (1976), Likert (1961) and others emphasise the importance of both task orientation and consideration/social support in achieving group goals. The effective mentoring relationship similarly requires a mixture (often shifting with the needs of the mentee) of task-focus (for which read challenge or stretching) and supporting behaviours (for which read nurturing). Authors such as Darling (1984) refer to both types of behaviours in their descriptions of what mentors do.

The stretching/nurturing dimension also reflects the complex duality of the goddess Athena – the real mentor in the Greek myth. She is at the same time the macho, fearsome huntress and the nurturing Earth Mother. Athena, who was closely associated with the owl as a symbol of wisdom, was frequently depicted in full armour and even was supposed to have been born fully armed! Yet she was also closely associated with handicrafts and agriculture. It is tempting to view these as masculine/feminine characteristics and some writers have done just that. However, in my experience, this can all too easily lead people into styles of mentoring behaviour based on gender stereotypes. The essence of effective mentoring is that mentors have the facility to move along the dimensions, in any direction, in response to their observation of the learner's need at the time.

The beauty of this model is its combination of simplicity and inclusiveness. All 'helping to learn' behaviours fit within these broad dimensions. ('Teaching' is not necessarily a helping to learn behaviour *per se* – being taught is something done to you, while learning is something you do yourself, or with someone else.) We can isolate five primary 'helping to learn' styles based on the dimensions (see Figure 3).

## Coaching

*Coaching* is a relatively directive means of helping someone develop competence. It is relatively directive because the coach is in charge of the process. Although there are, in turn, four basic styles of coaching, which range from the highly directive to more stimulative, learner-driven approaches, it is common for the learning goals to be set either by the coach or by a third party. In the world of work, coaching goals are most frequently established as an outcome of performance appraisal. The issue of learner commitment (is this really what matters to them?) is therefore relevant. Some of the useful behaviours effective coaches may display include challenging the learner's assumptions, being a critical friend and demonstrating how they do something the learner is having difficulties with.

## Counselling

*Counselling* – in the context of support and learning as opposed to therapy – is a relatively non-directive means of helping someone cope. By acting as a sounding-board, helping someone structure and analyse career-influencing decisions, and sometimes simply by being there to listen, the mentor supports the mentee in taking responsibility for his or her career and personal development.

## Networking

To function effectively within any organisation, people need personal networks. At the very least, they need an information network (how do I find out what I need to know?) and an influence network (how do I get people, over whom I have no direct control, to do things for me?). The same is true for the unemployed young adult in the context of community mentoring, for newly recruited researchers at university and people in many other situations, where mentoring can be applied. Effective mentors help their mentees develop *self-resourcefulness* by making them aware of the plethora of influence and information resources available to them – people, organisations and more formal repositories of knowledge. They may make an introduction to someone they already know, or talk the mentee through how he or she will make his or her own introduction to that person, or help the mentee build entire chunks of virgin network.

*Figure 3* **FOUR BASIC STYLES OF HELPING**

### Guiding

*Guiding (being a guardian)* is another relatively hands-on role and is the one most managers find easiest because it is closest to what they do normally. Giving advice comes naturally. It is unfortunate that so many managers, who have attended coaching courses or read well-meant books on the developmental role of the supervisor, come away feeling guilty, or worse, that they have to constantly restrain themselves from giving straight answers to their direct reports. The reality is that there are many situations where asking 'What do you think you should do?' is not an appropriate response. Using the tools of reflective analysis at inappropriate times is likely to have a far greater demotivating effect than simply leaving well alone. Equally,

however, always providing the answer isn't going to help someone grow. Because being a guide/guardian tends to carry with it
a relatively strong element of being a role model – an example of
success in whatever field the learner has chosen to pursue –
their behaviours, good or bad, are likely to be passed on to the
learner along with more practical support. At an extreme,
guardians become sponsors or godfathers, taking a very direct
interest in the learner's development, putting the learner forward for high-profile tasks, tipping him or her off about opportunities and actively moulding the learner's career. This can be
very stifling for the recipient, who may not be in a position to
resist this largesse, should the learner prefer to succeed by his or
her own resources. If learners comply with the mentors' manip-
ulations, a subtle psychological contract often emerges, in which
career progression is traded for loyalty and respect. Some cultures regard this more positively than others.

### Mentoring

Finally, *mentoring* draws on all four other 'helping to learn'
styles. Indeed, the core skill of a mentor can be described as
having sufficient sensitivity to the mentee's needs to respond
with the appropriate behaviours. Thus, the effective mentor
may use the challenging behaviours of stretch coaching at one
point and the empathetic listening of counselling a short while
later.

Where an organisation, or a national culture, or a mentoring
pair decide to draw the boundaries of what is appropriate behaviour for a mentor may vary substantially. What we call *developmental mentoring* assumes a diamond across the middle of the
diagram (Figure 4). Traditional US mentoring, by contrast, is
concentrated on a circle centred in the top right-hand corner
(Figure 5), and often encompasses a high level of sponsoring
behaviours.

## Mentoring as reflective space

On average, knowledge workers cannot acquire greater than 10
minutes at a time to focus without interruption on a specific
task or issue. Although people are often working longer hours
than a decade ago, they have less and less time to stop and
think deeply. In experiments with hundreds of managers and

*Figure 4* **DEVELOPMENTAL MENTORING**

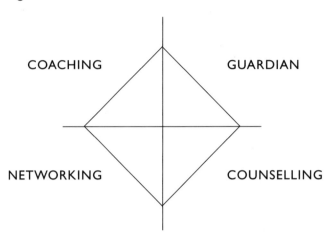

*Figure 5* **SPONSORING MENTORING**

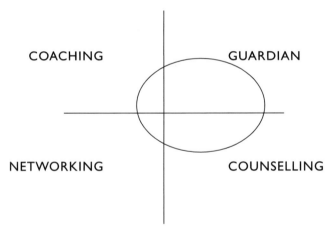

professionals, less than 3 per cent claim to find their deep thinking time at work, and of these, the majority do so by coming in very early in the morning. For most people, however, deep thinking time happens on the journey to and from work, in the bath or shower, taking exercise, doing the ironing, lying awake at night, or in other parts of their 'free' time.

Deep, reflective thinking is as essential to the effectiveness of our conscious brain as REM sleep is to our unconscious. In both cases, we become dysfunctional if our minds do not carry out the essential task of analysing, structuring, organising and storing. When we allow ourselves to enter *personal reflective space* (PRS), we put the world around us largely on hold. (Even if we are doing a complex physical movement, like jogging, or driving the car, we allow our internal autopilot to take over.) Often unbidden, although with practice it is possible to control the process, one issue of concern rises to the surface of our consciousness and we start to examine it with a depth and clarity we have not previously been able to apply to it. There are many comparisons for this process – I like the analogy of the mine disposal engineer gingerly examining a sea mine washed ashore. Another analogy is peering through the windows of a doll's house before gradually disassembling it. Whatever metaphor you use, the process is the same: you ask yourself questions about the issue in an attempt to better understand it and its impact on you. The more questions you ask from different perspectives, the more likely you are to achieve some level of insight, which allows you to position the issue very differently and consider new ways of dealing with it.

For me, a remarkably high proportion (more than 40 per cent) of excursions into reflective space result in being able to combine two difficult and until then separate situations in a way that achieves a positive outcome for both. Some people find that PRS takes them to a better understanding of the dynamics of their situation and gives them the confidence to take actions they had been avoiding. Possibly everyone is different, but there are at least two factors common to everyone who enters PRS regularly.

1  They emerge with renewed energy to tackle the issue they have been considering.
2  Whether vocalised or not, the person has been having a dialogue with him- or herself. (This is *not* a sign of madness, I hasten to add.)

When you engage in similar dialogue with a mentor, you are in effect inviting them to join you in your PRS. The dialogue becomes a trialogue, with the mentor asking you similar questions, but more rigorously, more objectively, from a wider range of perspectives, and more intensively. The effective mentor therefore takes you down the path from analysis, through under-standing and insight to plans for action in a faster, more thor-ough manner.

---

### AN EXAMPLE

The owner/manager of a 65-employee company was forced by a minor but significant health warning to consider throttling back on his hours and responsibilities. He was frustrated, however, by a complete failure to delegate key tasks to his three direct reports. After a while, he gave up, until the next heart twinge brought the issue back to the fore. This time, he sought help, asking a mentor to help him think the issues through. The mentor asked the kinds of question that put the behaviours of both sides into perspective – a set of unconscious collusions that would always result in problems being passed up to the boss. Whatever the conscious expectations the owner and his managers had of each other, the unconscious ones were those driving both sides' behaviour. Teasing these expectations into the open allowed the owner to design and implement a whole new range of tactics, which broke the fixed, negative cycle of behaviour and changed the relationship with two out of the three managers. (You can't win all the time!) One solution was to stop getting angry when the managers asked him to take a decision within their authority. Instead, he now patiently explained what they should do. When they arrived back at their office, however, they found an invoice 'For doing your job' and an appropriate sum deducted from their departmental budgets!

---

## Mentoring in the spectrum of learning

We have already pointed out the distinction between learning and teaching, but Table 1 offers a slightly different perspective. It is based upon developmental mentoring as opposed to a more sponsoring style.

Table 1 is sufficiently clear not to need a great deal of elabo-ration, but a few comments may be helpful. First, really good teachers are able to operate across the spectrum, although the structure and organisation of modern school systems makes it increasingly difficult for them to do so. Second, each of these approaches is both valid and valuable, but they represent a spec-trum from the highly impersonal to the highly customised and personal. Third, one can also plot an evolution in the quality of

## Table 1

| Role | Relationship | Dominant style | Affinity | Learning transfer | Power management |
|------|-------------|----------------|----------|-------------------|------------------|
| Teacher | Pupil | Tell | Aloof | Explicit data | High exerted power (parental) |
| Tutor | Student | Discuss | | | |
| Coach | Learner | Demonstrate/ give feedback | | | |
| Mentor | Colleague | Encourage | Close | Intuitive data | Low exerted power (collegial) |

the learning, in two ways. One is that the closer one gets to mentoring, the more the learning is shaped and encapsulated by the individual's own experiences. The other is the cascade from data, through information (a product of teaching), knowledge (tutoring), and skill (coaching) to wisdom (mentoring). At each stage of this cascade, the level of usefulness increases: data becomes interesting (except to train-spotters) only when it is organised into information; information allows people to pass examinations, but it requires further structure and context to turn it into knowledge, at which point it can be applied more widely. Having the knowledge of what a good manager should do doesn't mean that you are any good at it, however. For that, knowledge has to be applied and re-applied until it becomes skill. Finally, wisdom is the ability to apply accumulated knowledge and skill more widely again, having the judgement to draw meaningfully on experience in one or more situations to completely new contexts.

The implications of this for mentors are considerable. Whose wisdom are we talking about? Effective mentors tend to treat their wisdom like a nuclear arsenal – they very rarely let it fly. Instead they use their experience to inform the questions they ask and to challenge assumptions the mentee may be making. They also recognise that the greatest value to the mentee is to develop his or her own wisdom, not to borrow that of the mentor. Inevitably, in a successful and enduring mentoring relationship, there will be nuggets of observations by the mentor that the mentee will savour and perhaps pass on in turn, but the prevailing message of developmental mentoring is, 'Look into your own experience. Learn your own lessons. Build your own wisdom.' (This is heavily in contrast with the sponsorship mentoring view of, 'Listen to my experience. Learn from my triumphs and mistakes. Value my advice and judgement.')

## Coaching v mentoring

Given the frequent confusion between these two terms, it is worth drawing out the differences more finely. While coaching and mentoring share some tools and approaches, coaching is primarily focused on performance within the current job and emphasises the development of skills. Mentoring is primarily focused on longer-term goals and on developing capability. Table 2 puts more flesh on these bones.

*Table 2*

| Coaching | Mentoring |
|---|---|
| Concerned with task | Concerned with implications beyond the task |
| Focuses on skills and performances | Focuses on capability and potential |
| Primarily a line manager role | Works best off-line |
| Agenda set by or with the coach | Agenda set by the learner |
| Emphasises feedback to the learner | Emphasises feedback and reflection by the learner |
| Typically addresses a short-term need | Typically a longer-term relationship, often 'for life' |
| Feedback and discussion primarily explicit | Feedback and discussion primarily about implicit, intuitive issues and behaviours |

## Summary

This has been a very short introduction to fundamental but relatively straightforward ways of thinking about and describing the mentoring phenomenon. There are other descriptive models well worth a look – in particular, Carter's (1994) notion of mentoring contexts – and some of these are to be found in the recommended further reading. From my experience, however, the three models described in this chapter provide a very effective means of focusing both mentor and mentee on pragmatic expectations, both of each other and of the mentoring process.

# 4  HOW FORMAL SHOULD YOUR MENTORING SCHEME BE?

Not long ago, a petrochemicals company asked me to examine its two pilot, high-profile mentoring schemes – why weren't they working? Although launched with great enthusiasm and a considerable effort to train mentors, many of the relationships had simply never taken off. Others had faded away, often because the pair had run out of interesting things to talk about.

The problems stemmed from a variety of failings, not least insufficient clarity about roles and objectives. However, one of the most interesting results of our analysis of data gathered through focus groups was that the relationships that worked best and most often were generally those where the mentees themselves selected their mentors. Those relationships where the mentors were effectively imposed by the organisation were less effective and less likely to be continuing. This distinction was particularly marked among a group of high-flyers, who had one mentor of each kind, with the allocated mentor being from the same general area of the business and the personally selected mentor coming from another department.

Yet I know from experiences in other companies that encouraging people to select mentors entirely at their own choice leads in a high proportion of cases to relationships that deliver few, if any, benefits. Left to their own devices, people often choose someone they get on with extremely well and have known for a long time; or they approach a more senior high-flyer with a view to hanging on to their coat-tails. In the first case, while there is high rapport, there is typically very little opportunity for learning – growing pearls of learning requires at least some measure of grit in the oyster. When the chosen mentor is a high-flyer, he or she is often disinterested in helping to develop others; even if the high-flyer is interested, he or she is unable to create the necessary time.

It's as a result of this kind of contradiction in experience that emerging best practice in dealing with selection and matching centres around 'guided choice'. This can mean providing the mentee with strong guidance on how to find and use a mentor; or it can involve giving a limited number of options, selected by the scheme co-ordinator against criteria, which the mentee has provided or at least been involved in. The second of these approaches requires an existing pool of people who have volunteered and ideally been trained to be mentors.

There is, however, an even bigger conflict about mentoring, which is starting to be resolved and to which I referred in passing in Chapter 2. Put briefly, while most practitioners – both in-company and consultants – maintain that formal mentoring (ie a structured programme in which mentoring relationships are established and supported) is far more effective than informal, most academics, particularly in the USA, say that their studies show the opposite to be true. The clash between scientific observation and the experience of practitioners is not unique to mentoring – it happens in almost every aspect of endeavour – but understanding the reasons for the differences almost always stimulates a leap forward in practical implementation. And that is what is beginning to happen in mentoring right now.

## The arguments for formal mentoring

### Social inclusion

The main arguments in favour of a formal structure for mentoring centre around the need for some control of a process that, left alone, may not always work to the advantage of the organisation or the majority of the people in it. Social inclusion is an issue of increasing importance in most large organisations – how do we ensure both equal opportunities and the effective use of the diversity of talent, experience and backgrounds of our people? There are many well-documented cases of programmes aimed at a specific group, breaking the glass ceilings in gender, race or disability. The Cabinet Office, for example, runs a highly successful mentoring scheme aimed at people with severe physical (and sometimes mental) disability, who have ambitions to progress. The mentors are all very senior civil servants who see the relationship as a stimulating challenge.

Some of the most dramatic figures on mentoring for social inclusion come from the programme Big Brothers, Big Sisters, which links young people at risk in North America (and more recently in the UK) with a mentor in the community. The 10–16-year-old mentees in this programme are:

☐ 46 per cent less likely to begin drug abuse (70 per cent for minorities)

☐ 27 per cent less likely to begin underage drinking

☐ 30 per cent less likely to hit someone else.

They also skip 80 per cent fewer school days than non-mentored peers and have better relationships with parents, peers and teachers.

By contrast, informal mentoring appears to reinforce social exclusion because the scarce pool of mentors tends to be snapped up by those who are from the dominant social group, who are better educated and more obviously ambitious. In Europe and North America, this means that white male graduates are far more likely to find an informal mentor than any other group. Because mentor and mentee are so similar, an additional negative is that relatively little learning takes place on the part of the mentor. Diversity in a mentoring relationship stimulates examining issues from different perspectives.

## Positive mentoring

Formal mentoring also helps ensure that the relationship has clear purpose. The main reason why so many mentoring relationships fail is that neither mentor nor mentee is quite sure what they are aiming for, so there is no sense of direction. A formal scheme provides an umbrella purpose for the organisation, which helps mentor and mentee establish more specific goals for their own relationship.

Formal mentoring also ensures that there is a practical framework of support for mentor and mentee, including initial training and, in good practice environments, some form of continuing review, where mentors can address any further skills needs they identify. Training ensures both parties understand what is expected of them – not least who manages the relationship and what the boundaries are.

The formal process also helps to weed out 'toxic' mentors.

People who have manipulative goals, who represent values the organisation is trying to move away from, or who have so many problems of their own that they end up transferring these to the mentee are all common characters who can damage both the mentee and the organisation and who may actively seek to find mentees in an informal environment.

## The arguments for informal mentoring

A variety of highly analytical studies, mostly in the USA, suggest that people in informal mentoring relationships are much more satisfied with them. Among the reasons suggested for this are:

☐ Informal relationships take longer to get off the ground and tend to last longer overall, so there is more opportunity to create strong trust and to achieve medium-term goals. Formal relationships are often under considerable time pressure.

☐ Informal mentors are less likely to be in the role out of some form of obligation; they are there because they want to be. (There is evidence that altruistic mentors are less effective than those who see benefits for themselves in the relationship.) Many companies with formal schemes put subtle pressure on managers to become mentors as a way to demonstrate their commitment to people development.

☐ Informal mentors tend to have better communication and coaching skills than formal. (This is a matter of numbers – formal schemes often create increased demand that can be filled only by relaxing the competence criteria. In informal mentoring, the people most likely to put themselves forward – toxic mentors excepted – are those who have confidence in their own competence to perform the role.)

Broadly, these studies suggest that informal mentors offer stronger elements of friendship and empathy than formal mentors. Most of the other differences identified relate to the mentor's willingness to act as a sponsor to the mentee – something seen as a positive in traditional US mentoring, but as a practice to avoid in European, developmental mentoring, which places much more emphasis on helping the mentee become more self-resourceful.

## Summary

Getting the best from a mentoring scheme, then, involves building in the best aspects of both formal and informal approaches. A formal structure is essential because it provides meaning and direction for relationships and support where necessary. But individual relationships will flourish best when allowed to operate as informally as possible. Successful formal relationships very frequently go on to become successful informal ones.

An organisation that manages to create a mentoring/coaching culture can increasingly relax the level of formal intervention it imposes. What structures it does provide, in terms of educational materials and training, for example, become regarded as support mechanisms rather than controls. Meetings between mentors to develop their skills can become informal, self-driven support networks. And the range of people from whom the mentees learn can gradually be extended as they learn to build and manage their own learning nets.

# 5  WHO BENEFITS FROM MENTORING?

In the context of the business organisation, there are four principal beneficiaries of successful mentoring:

- the mentee
- the mentor
- the organisation itself
- (often forgotten) the mentee's immediate line manager or supervisor.

In this chapter we examine mentoring from the perspective of each of them, looking at the potential downsides as well as the advantages of having a mentor.

## Benefits to the organisation

Every company needs some form of career development programme to produce a succession of motivated, upward-moving employees. Even employees who are destined to remain at the same level may need career development as the jobs they are in change or become obsolete. Managers with high potential should identify and improve their skills, set career goals and know how to achieve those goals in the most practical and efficient way. Conventional career development courses provide some of the answers, but all too often fail to provide adequate follow-up. The results, too, are often hard to define. Schemes involving selection by assessment centres of high-flyers or frequent job rotation to gain wide experience probably offer the nearest thing to tangible results, but are extremely expensive, not least because at each change the young person has to start again at the beginning of the learning cycle of the new job.

Leaving career development solely to managers, while cheaper, tends to be singularly ineffective. A manager may lack the ability to recognise a potential high-flyer or, if he or she does, be reluctant to lose that employee by counselling him or her to move to another area of the company. Managers who are unavailable, uncommitted, or who dislike particular subordinates can effectively block the career paths of talented employees and prevent them from realising their potential.

A mentoring programme, as a formal method of recognising talent in a company, is a viable alternative to both these approaches. It can be carried out in tandem with traditional career development methods and has reasonably good predictability in its results. It may be run for as long as the employee benefits from it. As in many other relationships, both mentee and mentor have to work hard to make it succeed; both can draw substantial benefits.

Mentoring can work in most organisations, regardless of size, culture or market sector. It can communicate to employees far more fully the complexity of procedures and the unique nature of the company than any formal training course, induction booklets or company manual.

Mentoring enhances the abilities of both the mentor and mentee, so the organisation gains through increased efficiency. Companies with formal, longstanding mentoring programmes claim tangible increases in productivity and efficiency. Intangible benefits include improved staff morale, greater career satisfaction and swifter getting up to speed when mentored managers are inserted into a new job.

Another significant impetus behind mentoring is the cost – not in cash terms (mentoring is *not* a cheap alternative when you take into account the value of management time) – but in saving expensive off-site courses, which take employees away from productivity activity for weeks on end.

The primary rewards to a company of a mentoring programme are:

☐ easier recruitment and induction
☐ improved motivation
☐ management of corporate culture
☐ leadership development
☐ improved communications.

### Easier recruitment and induction

A formal mentoring programme eases the sometimes difficult process of assimilating new recruits. Companies such as BAe Systems and National Grid, for example, have found graduate induction has become less of an ordeal since they began mentoring. Enthusiasm has been productively channelled and graduates are taking on greater responsibility as their commitment grows.

Most staff turnover occurs during the first six months with a new employer and a major cause is inability to adjust rapidly enough. Assigning a mentor to a new arrival helps overcome the counterproductive problems of culture shock and the uncertainty most people feel as they find their feet in the new environment. Employees become productive more quickly and are likely to stay with the company longer.

Mentoring also cultivates in the mentee an increased sense of commitment and loyalty to the organisation. The mentor is the mediator between the mentee and the company. Through close interaction with the mentee, the mentor creates a personal atmosphere in what might otherwise seem a faceless bureaucratic organisation. The mentee receives through the mentor a positive perception of the company. The mentee can be made to feel he or she is participating in the inner operations of the company and this in turn generates a closer identification with the organisation's goals.

Many companies experience difficulties in attracting the right kind of graduates, even in times of severe unemployment. Even top financial services companies in the City of London are finding that graduates – and especially those with advanced degrees – will turn down employers who don't offer a mentoring programme. A mentoring programme can be a significant inducement for graduates to join less glamorous firms or industries because it demonstrates commitment to management development and staff retention. It is particularly attractive if it offers a fast track to middle management.

In some cases, a mentoring programme starts working for the company even before the new recruits turn up. Jewel Companies, a Chicago food retailing firm, designed a mentoring programme to 'merchandise an unglamorous retailer to bright young MBAs'. A spokesman explains:

Ours is a hard-working, long-hours kind of business – in other words, not the type MBAs looking for jobs would put on their list. We wanted to bring into the business a talent level we had not been able to reach. All MBAs expect the track to be fast. Now we can say to them: 'You will get enough attention in the first couple of years for both of us to know if you will succeed.' Using this strategy, we emphasise to MBAs that we groom fast-trackers.

More commonly, City firms and many IT companies now insist that all graduates and professional recruits have the opportunity to be mentored. They recognise that it is not just high-flyers who make a business succeed – many other people have a role to play and their development is equally important.

### Improved motivation

Mentoring can help reduce managerial and professional turnover at other critical stages, too. Young, ambitious people often undergo a period of frustration and impatience when they realise their progress up the company career ladder is slower than they initially expected. If mentees have a mentor who is taking an active interest in their career and who explains the reasons for and ways round current blockages, they are more likely to persevere. The mentor helps them understand and recognise the long-term plans the company has for them and helps the mentee make the most of the learning experiences inherent in the current job. Hence mentoring lessens the threat of other companies luring away promising young employees with offers of speedier career advancement.

A mentoring relationship also motivates the middle and senior managers involved and can be a valuable means of delaying 'plateauing'. A mentor is less likely to retire mentally in the job if he or she is constantly faced with fresh challenges arising from a mentoring relationship. Mentors are forced to clarify and articulate their own ideas about the company's organisation and goals in order to explain them to their mentees. They may feel they have to improve their own abilities to justify the mentee's respect. Cultivating potential in the company becomes a significant opportunity for the mentor to demonstrate that the old dog is still capable of learning and showing new tricks. As a result, mentors may find new purpose and interest in their jobs.

## Management of corporate culture

In the original edition, I titled this section 'A stable corporate culture'. Almost every mentoring programme I examined then had as part of its objectives passing on the nuances of the corporate culture. In the intervening 15 years, the emphasis has changed dramatically. Instead of preserving cultures, companies are desperately trying to change them. This poses a number of problems – not least that it makes it even more difficult to identify mentors with the 'right' values.

Mentor and mentee in an effective developmental relationship are able to explore the differences between espoused corporate values and actual behaviour. At the same time, the mentor helps to clarify in the mentee's mind which aspects of the culture are fixed and not open to challenge and which are open for dialogue. At one of the world's largest and most successful merchant banks, for example, new recruits soon learn that near-obsessive honesty is an immutable part of the culture, but that maintaining a work-life balance (on a par with integrity in the corporate values statement) is honoured more often in the breach. The mentee is able to use the mentor as a role model for selected aspects of the culture, while the mentor is able to use the mentee's constructive challenge to inform the continuing senior-level debate on how the culture should evolve.

## Leadership development

Besides teaching managerial and personnel skills, mentoring reveals to the mentee how power is gained and wielded within the company. This is frequently a crucial lesson and is one of the most powerful sources of motivation for a young manager. A business school education may teach valuable theoretical skills but it cannot normally teach a manager how to exercise and feel comfortable with power, nor can it give him or her the confidence to make a major deal on his or her own initiative, take calculated risks or launch a new product.

## Improved communications

The mentee's unique position in the organisation can aid informal communications because he or she straddles several levels. For example, through the relationship with the mentor the junior management mentee has access to and is accepted by middle management. At the same time he or she is accepted in the lower managerial levels. Since the mentee is familiar with the language and mannerisms of both, he or she can efficiently communicate each group's ideas and opinions to the other. Rich informal communication networks improve productivity and –efficiency in a company since they lead to more action, more innovation, more learning and swifter adjustment to changing business needs. It can be lonely at the top. The chance to pass information to lower levels of management restores interdependence between management levels and eases the flow of ideas and information. This special communication network also facilitates easier working of other areas of management development.

Mentoring can sometimes benefit an organisation in unexpected ways, too. In one company a mentee was being mentored with the ultimate objective of helping him leave. A spokesman explained:

> This highly talented individual has gone as far as is possible in this company. We have no appropriate position for him so we are grooming him to take over a small corporation outside this company. In the meantime, for the three to five years that he stays with us, we benefit from his productivity and enthusiasm. In the future we will have a very useful ally.

A similar case arose in the north-west region of ICI's engineering department. The company explains:

> A sponsored mechanical engineering student began training with us and met her mentor for about three hours on her first day. Two weeks later, she left us and decided to go up to university, forsaking her engineering ambitions. During this time the mentor had provided support, primarily in a counselling mode, to a person living away from home for the first time, in a strange environment. He helped her rethink her ambitions and come to a decision on her future.

The most recent large-scale study of mentoring programmes in the UK (Industrial Society 1995) found that the most common intention behind introducing a mentoring programme was to provide help and encouragement for those taking qualifications (56 per cent), followed by familiarising new recruits with the organisation (50 per cent), 'providing growth for any employee who requests a mentor' (46 per cent), developing senior managers (31 per cent) and fast-tracking (31 per cent). A handful of schemes addressed issues of equal opportunities.

The previous Industrial Society study in 1990 also looked at other factors, such as retention and identification of potential, both of which were important in the decision to launch a programme. The primary reason, however, was typically to support a programme of self-development.

Another study, this time from North America (CMSI 2001), asked programme co-ordinators how satisfied they were with the return on investment from mentoring. Some 52 per cent said they were moderately satisfied, and 29 per cent said they were highly satisfied.

### Improved retention of employees

Keeping the good people you have is increasingly being regarded as a core competitive advantage. In the war for talent, any reduction in employee turnover is a major benefit and mentoring has been shown to play a major positive role in retention.

A key indicator is 'intention to quit'. US studies of employees in large companies indicate that 35 per cent are thinking of leaving within the next 12 months. However, amongst those who have a mentor, the figure falls to 16 per cent. When it comes to actual resignations, the figures are even more startling. In SmithKlineBeecham's finance division, staff turnover in 1999 was 27 per cent – except among people who had a mentor, where it was 2 per cent! Some allowance must be made in these figures for sample bias (people who have given up on the company are unlikely to seek a mentor within it) but that is only likely to have had a minor effect.

With graduates, opportunity to improve retention appears to lie in the transition period between the end of their formal induction and getting settled into their first supervisory job. Many mentoring schemes stopped when the graduate induction stopped. Good practice now seems to be to carry on for six months plus, to bridge this period of uncertainty and relatively low self-confidence.

## Benefits to the mentee

### Easier induction for those coming straight from university or moving to a new country

One mentor comments: 'Mentoring is a means of smoothing out graduates' transition from an educational environment – one of the major changes of their life – and enabling them to settle in more quickly.' According to the NHS in Wales, it 'provides exceptional opportunities and the unique status of having someone to trust in a bewildering environment', who can direct the mentee's learning opportunities.

A French mentee working in England stresses how important her mentor has been: 'My mentor has worked abroad and can speak French. He has helped me to adapt to the British way of life. The scheme has definitely helped me to settle into this country and the company.'

Chemical company Hoescht had a dozen or so British apprentices in its German operations. Although they had a tutor in the UK, they also assigned German mentors to relieve isolation and to provide career counselling.

### Improved self-confidence

The mentee gains a sense of self-worth and importance. The one-to-one relationship between the mentor and the mentee helps the latter feel that the company values him or her as an individual rather than as a cog in the managerial wheel. A mentor gives mentees (in particular graduates) undergoing frequent job rotation and management change a point of stability in what may seem an unpredictable environment. By helping them explore their own potential, the mentor also enables them to gain the self-knowledge necessary for well-founded self-confidence.

### Learning to cope with the formal and informal structure of the company

Through the mentor, the mentee learns about the formal culture of an organisation, its values, its company image, objectives and predominant management style.

The mentor advises the mentee on self-presentation and behaviour so that he or she can fit into the company's formal culture. Mentees learn how to promote themselves within the organisation, when to be noticed as an individual and when to be seen working collaboratively. In one large multinational, the primary aim of the mentoring scheme was to help 'invisible' people in the finance department manage their reputation within the organisation in general.

A mentee learns how to operate successfully within the

informal culture. The mentor helps the mentee work through the internal company politics by identifying the key decision-makers in the company and which executives have the real power. As one senior executive comments: 'If you do not know the rules of the game, you cannot operate. The only way to know these rules is to be invited by an insider to participate.'

### Career advice and advancement

A mentor can act as a role model – a tangible symbol of what the mentee can achieve in the future. As a role model, the mentor helps the mentee to focus career aspirations and turn them into realistic objectives. This is a double-edged sword, of course. The mentee has to beware he or she does not adopt the mentor's weaknesses as well as his or her strengths!

The mentee learns how to move quickly up the promotion ladder. When the mentor is more senior and more experienced in corporate politics, he or she can advise the mentee on which jobs to take and when to take them.

A female mentee in the social services was advised by her mentor to apply for a position she felt was unattainable. She comments: 'Before the internal interviews my mentor kept dropping my name to other senior administrative officers. He also frequently mentioned me to his own superior. Two other people in the department also applied for the vacancy. There was a woman on my level who had four years' experience and a man a grade higher. Everyone was very surprised when I got the promotion, since it was virtually unknown for someone of my age and experience to jump three levels.'

Sometimes the mentor may suggest a total reorientation of career direction and may recommend a decrease or increase in the pace of advancement. One young manager recalls his attitude before he had a mentor:

> I was never sure about the timing of my career; when I should try to move upward or when I should stay in one position. I thought I ought to understand a job completely before I applied for promotion. Then a senior executive took an interest in my career and told me that if I stayed too long in one job I would probably get stuck there since I would not be recognised as a high-flyer. He advised me to apply for a post two grades above my current one. I didn't think I'd get it, but I did.

In traditional US mentoring, the mentor acts as a kind of sponsor, increasing the visibility of the mentee at executive levels by frequently describing how well his or her charge is progressing. The mentor may involve the mentee in his or her own projects and bring the mentee into executive meetings, inviting him or her to speak up. The mentor will brief the mentee beforehand on how to behave and give background on other subjects scheduled to be discussed.

Within the context of developmental mentoring, the mentee gains a sounding-board who will help also him or her think through the decision-making process, through which the mentee selects between career options. The mentor helps the mentee identify what he or she values and to assess each option against his or her personal values and goals. As a result, the mentee gradually becomes more self-confident in making career choices and more adept at turning down those that are likely to lead to blind alleys.

### Managerial tutorage

A mentee may gain an insight into management processes through observing his or her mentor closely. The mentor provides an example of effective management and successful leadership and so accelerates the mentee's learning pace. This will apply only where the mentor and mentee are close enough in location/function for the mentee to observe in the normal course of work – or when the mentor specifically invites the mentee to shadow him or her (for example, in making a presentation.) An American mentee at Unisys comments:

> A mentor teaches the invaluable lesson of people management to a mentee who is often straight out of management school. He may know all about cost-benefit analysis and be an economic wizard, but he needs to be shown, for example, the importance of building support teams. A mentor has the experience to teach this.

A British mentee agrees, explaining: 'When mentoring works, it minimises the period during which one learns from mistakes. As a graduate, you feed off someone else and so the learning processes are speeded up.' John Chadwick, formerly Director of Sundridge Park Management Centre, remembers his experience as a mentee at the Glacier Metal Company:

Before long we were exchanging notes on the shop floor experiences I was soaking in, comparing our assessment of abilities. All the time I was extending and testing my critical faculties. Towards the end of the session, he would always share with me his own problems and uncertainties. He would explain the process of resolving situations, the stress of decisions and the excellence of success. All the time he was infecting me with the management virus.

A mentor is able to use his or her knowledge of the organisation to facilitate the mentee's access to areas otherwise closed. As a result, the mentee better understands how the organisation functions. Interviews with 'graduated' mentees reveal that one of the most valuable parts of the relationship is frequent discussion of how the business works and why middle and senior management do not do things the way the mentee would. John Chadwick adds:

> As an engineer trained in logic, I found this world of compromise, choice and timing initially mysterious. Then, as my mentor's advice bore fruits, it became less of a mystery and more of a challenge to read the organisation. Rapidly I became able to discuss with him strengths and weaknesses in other managers, and ways in which they could be approached to form a working relationship. The blindly obvious shortcomings of the business seemed less idiotic when put by him into the context of the broader market.

My own experience of being guided in this way remains fresh in my mind, although it happened some 25 years ago. As a young junior manager in the publishers McGraw-Hill, I was convinced my boss's boss, the publisher, had no idea what he was doing. So many decisions he made appeared to be irrational. Then he retired and his successor took me under his wing. Although there was a reporting line through my boss, we developed a strong rapport, especially as we travelled together on sales calls to major advertisers. John spent much of the time asking me about my job, but also talked to me about his own role and the context of the decisions he had to make. After a while, I realised that his predecessor wasn't as stupid as I'd thought; he had simply been operating at a level of management more complex than I had previously been exposed to. As I understood this more deeply, I applied what I was learning to my own department, and soon found myself promoted. I had, in effect, graduated to a new level of thinking that opened new doors for me.

A mentee has a legitimate source of advice and information in the mentor. For example, Jenny Blake found:

> It was very difficult to sell to the Middle East, especially since I was a woman and not allowed to go there. My mentor was in charge of the Middle East marketing section and was able to give me invaluable advice. He made me aware of important cultural differences and expectations when I was dealing with foreign marketing representatives – for instance, how they expected to be treated with respect and to be made a fuss of.

A junior manager describes the problem he faced without such a figure: 'Often a young manager has to try to gather information without betraying his ignorance. It is a very risky business. To get ahead you have to supply the right answers and not ask the wrong questions.' In a mentoring relationship, the mentee can ask naïve questions in an unthreatening atmosphere. Helen Martin, a mentor at BP Chemicals, feels 'a mentor is not an agony aunt or a miracle cure for all problems. We are simply people who have probably experienced similar situations in the past. We can therefore help the individual to find the best way to tackle an issue themselves.'

### Benefits for the less talented employee

The less gifted employee who has the benefit of a mentoring relationship need not gain less from it. Their job satisfaction may be increased by an understanding of how to work within their limitations and how to broaden the current job, ie to seek challenge horizontally rather than vertically. They will need the same skills of handling people or of teamwork and the same knowledge of how the organisation functions to achieve lesser aims.

## Potential downsides for the mentee

Having a mentor isn't always a blessing. Mentors who want to relive their own careers through their mentee, who 'want to stop you making the mistakes I did' or who have their own agenda for the mentee, can be stifling. Indeed, there is some evidence that having an overbearing mentor is a relatively common cause for young graduates to move employer. Conflict between mentor and line manager in another context can sometimes spill over into the mentee's relationship with either or both; conversely, having a line manager and mentor who are too cosy can also leave the mentee feeling exposed and reluctant to be too open in mentoring discussions.

Although it is rare in developmental mentoring, in sponsoring mentoring it is common for the relationship to develop unhealthy levels of dependence and for mentor and mentee to end up competing with each other for positions.

Finally, mentors who are locked into advice-giving mode may sometimes give the wrong advice. Mentees need to have the personal strength and awareness to make their own mind up about what they should do, even if the mentor is unhappy about it.

In general, the downsides of mentoring for the mentee emerge only when the mentors are poor or the programme is poorly designed and/or implemented.

## Benefits to the mentor

All the surveys and reviews I have conducted in recent years to evaluate the outcomes of mentoring programmes have indicated that the most frequent and most powerful benefits for mentors are:

☐ the learning they take from the experience, both in having to explain intuitive reasoning and in listening to a different perspective (ie problems mentees have with their bosses often cause mentors to reflect on similar issues their direct reports may have with them!)

☐ the opportunity to take reflective space in a hectic daily schedule

☐ the satisfaction of knowing you have made a difference to someone else

☐ the intellectual challenge of working on issues for which you do not have to take personal responsibility and that may take you into unfamiliar territory.

Mentors questioned in the Industrial Society survey (1995) list the main benefits as prompting reassessment of their own views, leadership style, awareness of views of more junior staff, broader perspective and discovering talent. Other benefits recorded were 'useful role for plateaued managers' and good for their own career progression. Field experience suggests that when mentees are unaware of how much their mentors are getting out of the relationship, they are constrained in how much use they make of it.

### Improved job satisfaction

Grooming a promising young employee can be a challenging and stimulating experience for a mentor, especially if his or her own career has reached a temporary or permanent plateau. Some managers, whose careers have reached a real or perceived plateau, find the challenge of mentoring both rewarding and stimulating and have been motivated to put new effort into their own career planning.

Mentors often find the mentoring relationship rewarding in many other ways – for example, in the sense of pride when the mentee achieves personal goals. Mentors also gain a sense of purpose in seeing the values and culture of an organisation handed to a new generation and in thinking more carefully about company policies. Says an industrial company with a long-running mentoring programme:

> Mentoring has made us question traditional thinking and practices, firstly to clarify them in our own minds before explaining them to our mentees, but also in not just defending them when challenged through the innocent, unadulterated eyes of the newcomer who has not yet been influenced by our culture.

Mentors learn from the relationship, too. The process of climbing the corporate ladder often means missing out on new ideas, techniques and technologies. There never seems to be the time for catching up and at a certain stage it becomes embarrassing to admit ignorance. Directing the learning experiences of the mentee gives the mentor the excuse he or she needs to devote the time to developing his or her own knowledge, too. It is also often acknowledged that the best way to learn is to teach.

Some companies see mentees as a source of practical help for the mentor, while Midland Bank (now HSBC) has found that 'mentors have identified a need to increase their own business awareness of Midland Group in order to be better placed to respond to mentees'.

Some mentors use their mentees as 'robot arms' to accomplish at a distance and less publicly what they cannot do directly from their more visible position in middle or senior management. This applies particularly to information-gathering and the initiation of new projects. For some cultures this is tantamount to manipulation and not accepted as a valid aspect of the mentor's role.

Mentoring can give the mentor a different perspective on the company and keep him or her in touch with grassroots feelings.

Mentors often learn how to relate better with their own direct reports.

## *Increased peer recognition*

A mentor who identifies promising employees acquires a reputation for having a keen insight into the needs of the company. This enhances his or her status with peers.

The international accounting firm Merrill Lynch & Co has constructed a formal system of rewarding its mentors. Mentors' names are included in regularly circulated reports about mentees' accomplishments. Mentors are personally thanked by top management and are invited to be presenters at mentor briefing sessions, which are run for new participants. A spokesman for the firm explains: 'We feel we need to reward our mentors visibly and link their success publicly to the success of the mentoring programme.'

One thing the mentor does not receive, and should not be led to expect from the scheme, is a direct payment or bonus to compensate him for his time and effort. One argument against such payments is that developing others is an integral part of every manager's job. A more powerful argument is that mentorship has to be built on friendship and is a close and personal relationship. Hence, turning it into a paid service is likely to hinder the relaxed and informal atmosphere necessary between mentor and mentee. In theory, this can become a problem if the company links human development objectives to a bonus scheme as part of the annual performance appraisal. In practice, the trick is to ensure that the mentor is neither especially rewarded nor penalised for this part of his job.

A few companies reward their mentors with status, inviting them to attend annual or bi-annual lunches or dinners with top management, where people strategies are discussed in open forum. Access to top management thinking – the inside track – is a prized commodity in most organisations!

Mentors at Pilkington Glass, one of the earliest graduate mentoring schemes in Europe, perceived the following benefits:

☐ We clarify and question our perception of the company.

☐ We see the company through fresh eyes.

☐ We improve our abilities so we have more to offer the mentee.

☐ We see people work in different ways depending on whether they are theorists, activists etc.

☐ It offers a new challenge.

☐ It offers a new learning experience.

☐ We understand the trauma new recruits experience and can be more sympathetic to others undergoing change.

## Downsides for the mentor

As with the mentee, there are few significant downsides for mentors in carrying out the role, if they do it well, other than that this is yet another demand on their time. For this reason, I generally advise new mentors to think very carefully before committing to more than one or two relationships, or they may not do them justice. Some of the other downsides I have observed over the years include:

☐ breaking of confidentiality by the mentee (largely the mentor's fault)

☐ resentment from direct reports that they are not receiving similar time and effort invested in their development to that the mentor spends with the mentee

☐ loss of face when a succession of mentoring relationships fail (usually a sign of poor mentoring, but occasionally the result of a run of circumstances)

☐ having an overdemanding mentee (my favourite is the young graduate who came to see his mentor several times a *day* for reassurance – it took a threat by the mentor to throw the graduate through the window to stop this behaviour – by which time the relationship had nowhere to go!).

## Benefits to the line manager

It is surprising how little attention is paid to the line manager as a stakeholder in the mentoring relationship, yet he or she can make or break it. All too often, line managers only see the downsides of having a direct report mentored – the mentee will be taking more time away from his or her work for mentoring meetings, and *what are they saying about me?* The latter is a very valid concern. As a good working estimate, at least 90 per cent of mentoring pairs spend some time discussing the mentee's relationship with his or her boss. This seems to hold broadly true at all levels, from new recruit at the lowest levels to chief executive.

Where the line manager sees the positives, however, it benefits everyone. When the mentee can discuss relationships with his or her boss and other working colleagues within the mentoring meeting, it allows the mentee to put his or her own and other people's behaviour and expectations into perspective. The mentee develops, with the mentor's help, better strategies for tackling issues around these relationships. If the mentee has a difficult conversation to initiate, he or she can practise it first with the mentor. As a result, relationships between the line manager and the mentee, and between the mentee and other colleagues, can be substantially improved.

The line manager also has access to a second opinion. If he or she feels the mentee isn't understanding or committing to something important, the line manager can recommend the mentee to take it up with his or her mentor. It sometimes happens that the line manager sees this as a great opportunity to dump all that troublesome development stuff on someone else. This is a wasted opportunity that could be used to invest more time into the coaching role and raising the performance of the whole team.

## Summary

Listing the benefits of mentoring is useful in developing the general argument in favour of the process. There is a deeper reason, however, for developing a clarity about the expected outcomes of any mentoring programme. Where people have high clarity about the organisation's expectations from a mentoring programme, they are more likely to be clear about the objectives of their own relationship and this, in turn, appears to lead to more productive pairings. As we shall examine in subsequent chapters, knowing what you want out of mentoring is critical to getting what you want!

# 6 SELECTING AND MATCHING MENTORS AND MENTEES

It may seem an obvious point that mentors and mentees should be selected (or encouraged to come forward) within the context of the programme objectives. The qualities that are relevant for mentors and mentees in a programme aimed to help at-risk teenagers are not the same as those for people engaged in a mentoring programme aimed at people undertaking their first general manager job overseas. Yes, there will be generic similarities – for example, the mentees' need to understand and come to terms with their respective environments and the mentors' need to be able to empathise with the situations the mentee describes – but the circumstances and the purpose of the relationship defines the need in terms of expected behaviours and competencies.

Mentoring is a disciplined process, although it has few rules. The organisation should decide and explain carefully who it wants to mentor and why, the criteria for selection, and who will do the selecting. The criteria will vary from company to company but should always be drawn against the background of this question: 'How much will this person gain from a mentoring relationship?'

In this chapter we explore some of the generics and set out some principles for managing selection and matching processes.

## Choosing mentors

In theory, at least, the mentee should be the starting point for selecting the mentor. In practice, some organisations have begun by creating a pool of mentors and gone looking for suitable mentees for them (or sent them off to find their own!). This has the disadvantage of creating some level of obligation to find a mentee for any would-be mentor, no matter how incompetent they may be in the role, and risks making the whole process mentor-driven.

Every manager's job should entail a significant amount of developing other people and indeed some companies make it a virtual condition of each manager's advancement. In practice, however, some people are better cut out for it than others. Moreover, the ability to act as a mentor will often vary according to the manager's own stage of career development. For example, someone seeking or undergoing a major change in their own career development may not have the mental energy to spare for someone else's issues.

In selecting the mentor, a company must have a clear sense of the qualities that make a good developer of other people's potential. These qualities may differ from company to company, even from division to division. Equally, the ideal mentor for one person may be a disaster for another. It follows, naturally, that companies will disagree on the criteria they use to identify good mentors. Gerald O'Callaghan, formerly responsible for BP Chemicals' mentoring scheme, states:

> Mentors are not picked for any superhuman qualities – though some may fall into that category. Most are experienced, well-balanced professionals and managers who are interested in developing young people and broadening their own contribution to the company. They are among the best staff we have.

There have been numerous attempts to define the competencies of a mentor, most of them flawed by a failure to define to begin with what role is being measured. There is also a great deal of confusion in the literature between practical skills or competencies (what mentors do/how they do it) and functions/outcomes (the results of the mentoring relationship). My own view of the skill set has evolved significantly over the years and is now most succinctly summarised in Figure 6.

*Figure 6* **THE 10 MENTOR COMPETENCIES**

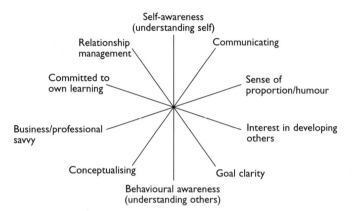

[*The following section on the 10 mentor competencies is taken from Clutterbuck (2000a) and is reproduced with kind permission of the publishers, the Association for Management Education and Development.*]

## 1 Self-awareness (understanding self)

Mentors need high self-awareness in order to recognise and manage their own behaviours within the helping relationship and to use empathy appropriately. The activist, task-focused manager often has relatively little insight into these areas – indeed, he or she may actively avoid reflection on such issues, depicting them as 'soft' and of low priority. Such attitudes and learned behaviours may be difficult to break.

Providing managers with psychometric tests and other forms of insight-developing questionnaire can be useful *if they are open to insights in those areas.* However, it is easy to dismiss such feedback, even when it also comes from external sources, such as working colleagues.

Some managers actively seek psychometric analysis, yet fail to internalise it – to carry out the inner dialogue essential to carrying knowledge through to action. Not that all personality insights should necessarily lead to action; in many cases, the role of internal dialogue may be to help the person accept that a behaviour pattern or perceived weakness can reasonably be lived with.

Interviews with mentors and mentees indicate that having some level of personality and motivational insight is useful for building rapport in the early stages of a relationship. 'This is me/this is you' – is a good starting-point for open behaviours.

People who have low self-awareness can be helped in a number of ways. One is through dialogue with a trained counsellor/facilitator, helping them relate psychometric and other behavioural feedback to specific actions and behaviours. By learning how to think through such issues for themselves, they may become more effective at doing the same for others.

Figure 7 shows a useful way of looking at this kind of approach to building self-awareness.

### *Figure 7* **BUILDING SELF-AWARENESS**

**Personal strengths/ high aptitudes**

*What makes you succeed?*

*What prevents you from succeeding? What causes you to fail?*

Drives ———————————————————————— Fears

*What would you like to be better at?*

*What do you lack the confidence to tackle?*

**Personal weaknesses/ low aptitudes**

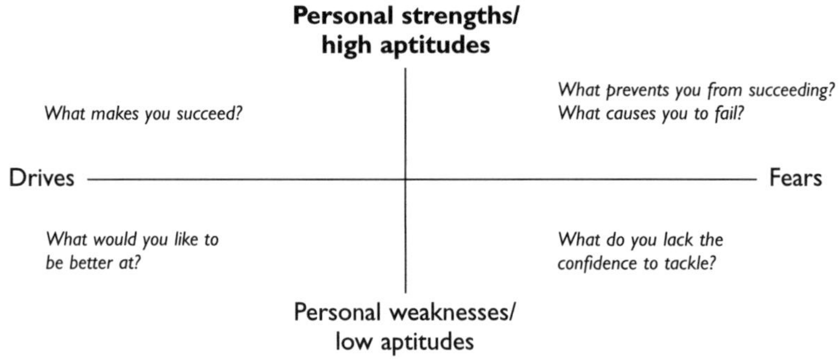

If nothing else, the model helps open up some of the hidden boxes in the Johari window!

An important debate here is whether low self-awareness is the result of low motivation to explore the inner self (disinterest), or high motivation to avoid such exploration, or simply an inability to make complex emotional and rational connections (in which case there may be physiological aspects to consider as well). The approach in helping someone develop self-awareness will be different in each case and is likely to be least effective in bringing about personal change.

### 2 Behavioural awareness (understanding others)

Like self-awareness, understanding how others behave and why they do so is a classic component of emotional intelligence. To help others manage their relationships, the mentor must have reasonably good insight into patterns of behaviour between individuals and groups of people. Predicting the consequences of specific behaviours or courses of action is one of the many practical applications of this insight.

Developing clearer insight into the behaviours of others comes from frequent observation and reflection. Supervision groups can help the mentor recognise common patterns of behaviour by creating opportunities for rigorous analysis.

### 3 Business or professional savvy

There isn't a great deal to be done here in the short term – there are very few shortcuts to experience and judgement. However, the facilitator can help the potential mentor understand the need for developing judgement and plan how to acquire relevant experience.

Again, the art of purposeful reflection is a valuable support in building this competence. By reviewing the learning from a variety of experiences, the manager widens his or her range of templates and develops a sense of patterns in events. The more frequently he or she is able to combine stretching experience with focused reflection – either internally or in a dialogue with others – the more substantial and rapid the acquisition of judgement.

A useful method of helping people develop business savvy is to create learning sets, where a skilled facilitator encourages people to share their experience and look for patterns.

### 4 Sense of proportion/good humour

Is good humour a competence? I would argue strongly that it is. Laughter, used appropriately, is invaluable in developing rapport, in helping people to see matters from a different perspective, in releasing emotional tension. It's also important that mentor and mentee should *enjoy* the sessions they have together. Enthusiasm is far more closely associated with learning than boredom is!

Can adults develop a good sense of humour if they do not already have one? Probably not easily. However, a good deal of pessimistic attitude and cynicism derive from a feeling of disempowerment and a perception of lack of control over one's circumstances. Such attitude changes can be created by helping people become more at ease with themselves, with their role in the organisation and their potential to influence their environment. The most obvious way to make that happen – apart from wholesale culture change within the organisation – is for the individual to have his or her own mentor.

In practice, good humour is a vehicle for achieving a sense of proportion – a broader perspective that places the organisation's goals and culture in the wider social and business context. People acquire this kind of perspective by ensuring that they balance their day-to-day involvement with work tasks against a portfolio of other interests. Some of these may be related to work – for example, developing a broader strategic understanding of how the business sector is evolving; others are unrelated to work and may encompass science, philosophy or any other intellectually stimulating endeavour. In general, the broader the scope of knowledge and experience the mentor can apply, the better sense of proportion he or she can bring.

## 5 Communication competence

Communication isn't a single skill; it is a combination of a number of skills. Those most important for the mentor include:

- listening – opening the mind to what the other person is saying, demonstrating interest/attention, encouraging him or her to speak, holding back on filling the silences
- observing as receiver – being open to the visual and other non-verbal signals, recognising what is *not* said
- parallel processing – analysing what the other person is saying, reflecting on it, preparing responses; effective communicators do all of these in parallel, slowing down the dialogue as needed to ensure that they do not overemphasise preparing responses at the expense of analysis and reflection; equally, they avoid becoming so mired in their internal thoughts that they respond inadequately or too slowly
- projecting – crafting words and their emotional 'wrapping' in a manner appropriate for the situation and the recipient(s)
- observing as projector – being open to the visual and other non-verbal signals, as clues to what the recipient is hearing/understanding; adapting tone, volume, pace and language appropriately

☐ exiting – concluding a dialogue or segment of dialogue with clarity and alignment of understanding (ensuring message received in both directions).

Some tools to help develop these competencies are *neuro-linguistic programming* (if used with a sense of proportion) and *situational communication*. Situational communication, developed by the ITEM Group with help from Birkbeck College, helps people understand the communication requirements of different commonplace situations and focus on the development of specific skills in those situations. It thus has a very high utility factor. Alongside situational communication is a very practical method of diagnosing communication styles, which enables the individual to become more self-aware of his or her own style preferences and recognise the preferences of others. Good mentors will generally need a strong sense of situation and a high degree of adaptability between styles.

## 6 *Conceptual modelling*

Effective mentors have a portfolio of models they can draw upon to help mentees understand the issues they face. These models can be self-generated (eg the result of personal experience), drawn from elsewhere (eg models of company structure, interpersonal behaviours, strategic planning, career planning) or – at the highest level of competence – generated on the spot as an immediate response.

According to the situation and the learning styles of the mentee, it may be appropriate to present these models in verbal or visual form. Or the mentor may not present them at all – simply use them as the framework for asking penetrating questions.

Developing the skills of conceptual modelling takes time, once again. It requires a lot of reading, often beyond the normal range of materials that cross the individual's desk. Training in presentation skills and how to design simple diagrams can also help. But the most effective way can be for the mentor to seize every opportunity to explain complex ideas in a variety of ways, experimenting to see what works with different audiences. Eventually, there develops an intuitive, instinctive understanding of how best to put across a new idea.

### 7 *Commitment to their own continued learning*

Effective mentors become role models for self-managed learning. They seize opportunities to experiment and take part in new experiences. They read widely and are reasonably efficient at setting and following personal development plans. They actively seek and use behavioural feedback from others.

These skills can be developed with practice. Again, having a role model to follow for themselves is a good starting-point.

### 8 *Strong interest in developing others*

Effective mentors have an innate interest in achieving through others and in helping others recognise and achieve their potential. This instinctive response is important in establishing and maintaining rapport and in enthusing the mentee, building confidence in what he or she could become.

While it is possible to 'switch on' someone to self-advantage of helping others, it is probably not feasible to stimulate an altruistic response.

### 9 *Building and maintaining rapport/relationship management*

The skills of rapport-building are difficult to define. When asked to describe rapport, in their experience, managers' observations can be distilled into five characteristics:

- ☐ Trust:           Will they do what they say?
                     Will they keep confidences?
- ☐ Focus:           Are they concentrating on me?
                     Are they listening without judging?
- ☐ Empathy:         Do they have goodwill towards me?
                     Do they try to understand my feelings, and viewpoints?
- ☐ Congruence:      Do they acknowledge and accept my goals?
- ☐ Empowerment:     Is their help aimed at helping me stand on my own feet as soon as is practical?

To a considerable extent, the skills of building and maintaining rapport are contained in the other competencies already described. However, additional help in developing rapport-building skills may be provided through situational analysis – creating opportunities for the individual to explore with other people how and why they feel comfortable and uncomfortable

with them in various circumstances. This kind of self-knowledge can be invaluable in developing more sensitive responses to
other people's needs and emotions.

The mentor can also be encouraged to think about the con-
textual factors in creating rapport. Avoiding meeting on the
mentor's home ground (eg in his or her office) may be an obvious matter, but where would the mentee feel most comfortable?
Sensitivity to how the meeting environment affects the mentoring dialogue can be developed simply by talking the issues
through, both in formal or informal training and with the
mentee.

## 10 Goal clarity

The mentor must be able to help the mentee sort out what he
or she wants to achieve and why. This is quite hard to do if you
do not have the skills to set and pursue clear goals of your own.

Goal clarity appears to derive from a mixture of skills
including systematic analysis and decisiveness. Like so many of
the other mentoring competencies, it may best be developed
through opportunities to reflect and to practise.

In the first edition of this book, I incorporated a useful acronym
from a North American article, which maintained that the
mentor:

☐ **M**anages the relationship
☐ **E**ncourages
☐ **N**urtures
☐ **T**eaches
☐ **O**ffers mutual respect
☐ **R**esponds to the mentee's needs.

Once again, views have moved on. While the notion of the
mentor managing the relationship still holds favour in some US
companies, the wider global expectation is for the mentor to
assist the mentee in taking over the management of the relationship. Similarly, when it comes to responding to the mentee's
needs, it is no longer seen as a good idea for the mentor to be
more than minimally interventionist. Rather, the mentor helps
the mentee work out his or her own solutions. The concepts of

encouragement, nurturing, teaching and offering mutual respect remain largely unchanged, however, and we repeat those notes here (with minor amendments) for background information.

## The mentor who encourages and motivates

The ability to encourage and motivate is another important interpersonal skill that the mentor must have in abundance if the relationship with the mentee is to reach its full potential.

The mentor must be able to recognise the ability of the mentee and make it clear to the mentee that he or she believes in the mentee's capacity to progress within the company. The mentor must be willing to let the mentee turn to him or her for as long as needed, as well as be willing to help the mentee to eventually become independent.

The mentor encourages the mentee through recognising the different roles he or she can play. For a certain period the mentor can be a reassuring parental figure to whom the mentee can turn for support and sympathy. The mentor must also at this stage be willing to let the mentee identify with him or her and use him or her as a role model. At other stages of the relationship, the mentor can encourage the mentee to become more independent and make individual decisions.

One mentor in a civil service department recalls how difficult it was to learn this lesson:

> I had this intelligent individual who was highly motivated. I expected his progress to be extremely rapid, but was surprised to find that he seemed to depend on me for quite some time. I was worried about it and considered whether I ought to try to force him somehow to make his own decisions unaided by me. Eventually I decided to go at his pace and not the pace I expected. He is now at a higher level than me in the company, but recently came to me to thank me for not rushing him in that first year. He explained he had found it very difficult to adjust to his new job and had found the new pressure especially hard to cope with. Apparently, my support and encouragement had kept him going through it all.

The ability to encourage and motivate is an especially important skill for the mentor if, as we discussed in Chapter 5, the company has a deliberate policy of not promoting high-flyers until they have a broad base of experience. If these people are to be prevented from seeking faster promotion elsewhere, the mentor has to help them extract a high degree of job satisfaction from their experiences now and let them know they will reap the rewards for their patience later in their career.

One corporate mentor explains:

> We get so many MBAs coming straight from college who expect to race up the promotion ladder. Without a mentor to explain the system to them, few of them realise that this is just not the way we operate. If we discover a talented individual, we allocate them to different areas of the company before we promote them so that they understand and have been directly involved in all aspects of the business.

A young manager in a small British defence firm emphasises the point with reference to the difference the support of a senior manager made to his career:

> I graduated with an engineering degree and immediately took my MBA. I then successfully applied for the position of technical manager, which had just been newly created in a defence firm. I found my new job extremely difficult because I was dealing with engineers who were obviously far more experienced than I and whose technical knowledge far outmatched mine. They plainly resented my presence. A few were even openly hostile to me.
>
> Fortunately, since my position was new to the company itself, a senior manager had been asked to help me as much as possible. He supported and encouraged me. Sometimes it was only this which stopped me from leaving. More importantly, he helped me to recognise that my difficulties were not caused by my own incompetence or failure, as I had originally thought, but that in fact the engineers' hostility had another cause and was aimed at my position rather than at me personally. He explained that the company had been trying to get the structure of the technical side of the company more into line with central management. I was just unlucky to be caught in the middle of a war between management and the engineers.

Armed with the knowledge that he was fully supported by top management, this young manager was able to ride the storm until he won the respect of the engineering staff.

## The mentor who nurtures

The mentor must be able to create an open, candid atmosphere that will encourage the mentee to confide in and trust him or her. The mentor is there to draw out the mentee and help discover his or her identity within the organisation. With the help of the mentor, the mentee undertakes self-assessment and discovers where his or her skills, aspirations and interests lie. Most importantly, the mentor must be able to listen to the mentee and ask open-ended questions that will draw the less experienced person out.

One key test of the mentor who nurtures is a track record of bringing along subordinates. If his or her department has provided a consistent breeding-ground for talented young supervisors and managers, then the chances are high that he or she will make a good mentor for people from other departments.

## The mentor who teaches

This is a skill that the mentor may need to be taught, because being a really good teacher does not come naturally to many people. Highly ambitious, self-motivated people (and the description applies to most people who make it to top management) often lack the patience to teach. Yet the mentor must know how to help the mentee maximise his or her opportunities to learn. The mentor does this by creating a stimulating environment that consistently challenges the mentee to apply theory to the real world of management.

A mentor may teach his or her mentee using the following methods:

☐ The mentor holds 'what if?' sessions where he or she guides the mentee in problem-solving discussions to encourage him or her to discover as many alternatives as possible.

☐ The mentor discusses with the mentee real problems the mentor is currently dealing with or has recently dealt with. Rather than expand upon the cleverness of his or her own solutions, the mentor asks the mentee what course of action he or she would take. The mentor can often complete the analysis by telling the mentee the solutions he or she actually devised and why they were chosen. In this way, through mini internal case studies, the mentor gives the mentee an insight into decision-making in higher-level jobs.

☐ The mentor plays devil's advocate. In a protective environment, the mentor teaches the mentee how to assert his or her opinions and influence the listener in difficult situations. The mentor plays aggressive and threatening roles so that the mentee learns to handle stressful and potentially explosive situations. A vice-chairman in an advertising company was helped in his career by a senior executive in the corporation. This mentor invited opposition from his mentee and frequently acted in a domineering and brusque manner. The mentor's aim was to help develop in his mentee an aggressiveness that he considered was essential for success in that field. The vice-chairman comments:

> Before I met my mentor I was not particularly forceful. However, when I talked to him I found I had the choice either to be chewed up, or to assert myself. He constantly pushed me in these one-to-one confrontations so that now when I talk to a client I have developed a way of expressing my opinions with weight and force.

## The mentor who offers mutual respect

An essential ingredient in any mentoring relationship is mutual respect between the two partners. If the mentee does not respect and trust his or her mentor's opinions, advice and influence – and vice versa – the benefits from the relationship will be severely limited. Programme co-ordinators must remember that a mentee's attitude towards the mentor will incvitably be influenced by the mentor's general reputation within the company.

To be more precise, the mentee will:

☐ assess the mentor's professional reputation by scrutinising his or her past performance; if a mentor has been involved with too many failed projects the mentee is likely to feel that a close alliance with that person will do his or her career little good

☐ assess the mentor's interpersonal skills; for example, a mentee may feel that a rewarding relationship could not be established with a mentor who is heard of only through memos and telephone calls

☐ assess the mentor's status with his or her colleagues; if the mentor commands respect and esteem from peers, the mentee feels his or her career will benefit from being associated with the mentor

□ assess the mentor's corporate alliances; the mentee must believe that his or her mentor has enough influence in the organisation to make a tangible difference to his or her career.

This latter point illustrates yet again the evolution that has taken place in our thinking about mentoring since these words were first penned. The emphasis on career outcomes expressed here has now generally been balanced by an equal or greater emphasis on the personal development outcomes, which may or may not have a direct impact on career achievement. Respect within developmental mentoring comes less from an appreciation of what the mentor can do for the mentee than from what he or she can help the mentee do on his or her own.

---

### Checklist – ideal characteristics to seek in a mentor

Look for someone who:

□ already has a good record for developing other people

□ has a genuine interest in seeing younger people advance and can relate to their problems

□ has a wide range of current skills to pass on

□ has a good understanding of the organisation, how it works and where it is going

□ combines patience with good interpersonal skills and an ability to work in an unstructured programme

□ has sufficient time to devote to the relationship

□ can command a mentee's respect

□ has his or her own network of contacts and influence

□ is still keen to learn.

---

## The mentor from hell

The mentor from hell exists – at least in the minds of mentees who have been unfortunate enough to encounter him or her. Consider this story from a young manager, recalling his days as a graduate mentee:

Once every six months I'd be summoned to the great man's presence. I'd come slightly early and he would always be running late. I'd sit in the ante-room, where his secretary made sure I didn't steal any paper clips. As I was shown in, he'd always be putting away my file – reminding himself of who I was. Then he'd talk at me solidly for over an hour. Finally, he'd ask if I'd found it useful. I never had the courage to tell him the truth . . . !

This mentor hadn't a clue and probably didn't want to know how to do the job properly anyway; it might have spoiled the ego trip. He might have been horrified to be told that good mentors speak for less than 20 per cent of the time, address issues raised by the mentee, and expect to engage in quality dialogue on a much more frequent basis than once every six months.

Some other common toxic mentors include:

☐ people who rush around 'helping' others in order to avoid addressing their own issues and often end up transferring their problem into the mentee's situation
☐ people who have an alternative agenda
☐ people who take umbrage when the mentee adopts a different solution from the one they have proposed
☐ people who are not switched on to their own learning.

## Choosing mentees

'So what's the business problem?' That's the first question I typically ask when working with an organisation to design a mentoring programme, because without a clear target group with a specific issue to manage, it will be very difficult to establish whether the project has been worthwhile. Very often there is a mixture of objectives, but the most common seem to be:

☐ to retain key staff
☐ to overcome institutional barriers to progress for disadvantaged groups
☐ to build bridges between parts of the organisation
☐ to support culture change, especially after a merger or major acquisition
☐ to support a competency programme.

Defining the business (or community) issue largely defines the selection criteria for mentees, whether these are used to identify people through some central co-ordinating mechanism or to enable people to decide for themselves whether to apply. In the Cabinet Office's Disability Leadership Programme, for example, potential mentees nominate themselves but receive endorsement from their department and have to attend an interview process that selects those that will take part in the full scheme, complete with bursary, and those that will simply receive a mentor.

At high-tech company Araya (formerly Lucent) mentees nominate themselves onto a broad self-development programme whose members meet monthly to learn together. Although intended originally for high and low performers, the programme has attracted a wide range of people, each of whom is offered a choice of two mentors.

Mentoring schemes for high-flyers tend to have some element of evaluation built in to ensure that they have the commitment and potential to make effective use of the opportunity they have been given.

At Security Pacific National Bank in California, vice-president of personnel Bennett Dolin explains how his company learnt the importance of selecting mentees carefully. 'Where we had failures, the main reason was poor selection. Some people looked a lot better than they were. As they went through the programme, we realised they had no substance to match the appearance.' Dolin's company now carefully screens each applicant.

At National Westminster Bank, the mentoring programme encourages potential high-flyers to move onto the fast track at an early stage. Interested candidates undergo a series of rigorous tests and interviews. If they are deemed to have potential, they then attend a week-long training course where their potential is discussed and they are given practical suggestions for personal development.

Some ground rules, which have been learned the hard way in a wide variety of organisations (but that doesn't stop other companies repeating the mistakes), include:

☐ Don't assume that everyone in the target group wants to have a mentor. A large financial services company in the City dutifully followed orders from New York and set up mentoring pairs for all its middle-level women, matching them either with more senior women or male executives. In interviews, many of the women reported that they were bemused by the project. While they had had very pleasant lunches, neither they nor the mentors were clear about what the purpose of meeting was, and many felt patronised by what they saw as a heavy-handed approach. Others saw the initiative as some kind of mark of inferiority – 'Somebody has decided I have a problem, but they haven't the balls to tell me what it is,' said one woman.

□ Don't assume that any target group sees itself as a group. One company, concerned that hardly anyone had signed up for a mentoring programme for people from ethnic minorities, discovered that the intended beneficiaries saw themselves either in their professional status or from much smaller communities – Muslims and Hindus saw their issues as very different and resented being lumped together.

□ Accept that some people may have less need of a mentor at some points in their career than others. Giving the individual some say in when he or she becomes involved increases personal commitment to the process. (A recent example I encountered involved a small group of middle managers who had not met their assigned mentors more than once or twice over almost a year. When quizzed about their reluctance, they explained that the mentor was fine, but not currently needed. Each of them had an excellent and productive developmental relationship with their line manager and with the tutor on the leadership course they were taking. 'Right now, I'm concentrating on applying what I'm learning to my current job and my performance in a couple of skills areas,' explained one. 'I can't cope with any more help at the moment. But I'd expect to make use of my mentor when I need to put all this into the bigger picture and establish some longer-term development goals.')

□ Sometimes a mentor is not the most appropriate form of help. Until a few years ago, I would routinely recommend companies setting up mentoring for graduate entrants to provide a mentor from day one. Practical experience shows this is usually a mistake. It typically takes three to six months in the organisation before the mentee understands enough of the systems and culture to ask insightful questions, but by this time one or both parties has often become bored and the relationship struggles to get back on course. Organisations are increasingly opting instead for a six-month buddy system, where the graduate is teamed up with a recruit from the previous year who can show him or her the ropes.

## The effective mentee

At first sight, it may seem invidious to set out criteria for 'good' mentees. After all, surely the purpose of mentoring is at least partially to help people become more effective. However, how the mentee behaves can have a substantial impact on the quality and type of help he or she receives. Moreover, there is a surprisingly wide literature about what mentors are looking for in a mentee. Take the following analysis from the well-respected US author Michael Zey (1984):

☐ *Intelligence* – the mentee must be able to identify and solve business problems rapidly.

☐ *Ambition* – the mentee must be gifted and have the ambition to channel his ability into career advancement. The mentor also wants to further his career and looks for a mentee who will advance through the organisation with him.

☐ *Succession potential* – the mentor also wants a mentee who demonstrates that he is capable of performing the mentor's own job. The mentor wants to be sure that he has groomed a replacement.

☐ *Strong interpersonal skills* – the mentee must be able to make new alliances for the mentor as well as retaining the ones the mentor has already established.

A study carried out in the USA in 1982, but still not replicated or superseded, adds a further important, if somewhat obvious, characteristic. It found that employees who performed visible, risky and important tasks were three times as likely to form mentoring relationships of their own accord as those who took few risks. It suggests that mentor relationships succeed and are more mutually rewarding if the mentee is chosen for his or her general, all-round reputation for hard work, enthusiasm and ability.

This is the language of sponsorship mentoring rather than developmental mentoring. It assumes that mentoring targets only the elite of the business and should not be wasted on less capable people. Certainly, this is a view that has been increasingly challenged as companies perceive mentoring as a tool of far wider usage that can be directed at people of a wide range of abilities and ambitions.

Nonetheless, there is some validity in the concept of the 'good' mentee. Successful mentoring relationships (success is defined as occurring when one or both parties achieve significant learning and/or support) are characterised, among other things, by mentees who are:

□ realistically ambitious for the relationship, having clear expectations of what it can do for them

□ unambiguous about their own role in selecting and bringing issues for discussion

□ prepared to take the prime responsibility for meeting arrangements and the agenda

□ willing to challenge and be challenged

□ able to approach the relationship with respect, good humour and openness

□ aware of the obligations the relationship places on them, with regard to their behaviour towards the mentor and to interested third parties, such as their line manager.

The more closely the mentee meets these characteristics, the more he or she (and the mentor) is likely to get out of the relationship. By contrast, mentoring is often difficult to make work in cultures where a high proportion of people adopt an 'outer-directed' view of the world – ie they have low belief in their own capacity to influence events in their favour. Although mentoring relationships can flourish in such an environment, the mentor needs great patience.

Other studies of mentoring relationships, from Scandinavia, suggest that the most effective are those where the mentee is highly proactive and the mentor relatively reactive.

## Must the mentee share the same qualities as the mentor?

There is a common assertion that in order for a mentoring relationship to succeed, the mentee must have a similar personality to the mentor's. Elizabeth Alleman and her colleague Isadore Newman (Alleman *et al* 1984) attempted to establish whether a similarity of personality or background was indeed the basis of rewarding mentor relationships. Alleman and Newman studied 100 managers, 29 pairs reporting a mentoring relationship and 21 pairs reporting a typical business relationship. The two compared the relationship between the mentor and the mentee to the relationship between a manager and his or her superior. Through personality tests and questionnaires they discovered:

☐ Mentoring pairs have no more similarities in personality or background than non-mentored pairs. When participants described themselves and their partners, their profiles contained few shared traits.

☐ Mentoring relationships are not based on complementary personality traits. Newman and Alleman did not find evidence to support the suggestion that mentors choose mentees whose strengths and skills offset the mentor's weaknesses.

☐ Mentors do not believe there are any special similarities between themselves and their mentees.

☐ Mentees view their mentors as similar to ideal workers and identify with them to a greater extent than managers who have a non-mentoring relationship with their supervisor.

In short, Alleman and Newman demonstrate that it is not essential for the mentor and mentee to have similar personalities or backgrounds. Indeed, as we have seen, if a cultural re-adjustment is needed in the organisation, then it may pay to avoid deliberately too close a match.

In another more recent study of personality and mentoring, Engström (1998) examined 30 pairs of mentors and mentees within a Swedish multinational company. The pairs included all gender options except female to female. He based his analysis of personality on five factors, which he describes as 'generally accepted in the field of personality and [which] include most other personality factors presented in the field'. These are: extroversion, emotional stability, agreeableness, conscientiousness and openness to experience.

Among Engström's conclusions are that mentoring relationships are seen as most successful when:

- ☐ both mentor and mentee demonstrate high extroversion
- ☐ both demonstrate a high level of agreeableness (defined as encompassing likeability, friendliness, social adaptability, altruism, affection, compliance)
- ☐ the mentee demonstrates much greater conscientiousness than the mentor (ie the mentee assumes ownership of the process)
- ☐ in the mentee's perception, the mentee demonstrates high openness to experience and the mentor high emotional stability.

An unexpected conclusion from the research was that men-only mentoring pairs were always perceived by both parties as more successful than mixed gender pairs, whether the woman was mentor or mentee. (Without a female to female comparison, this conclusion should be treated with some caution, insofar as drawing any implications is concerned.)

## Matching mentors and mentees

One of the advantages of informal mentoring is that would-be mentees can have as many bites at the cherry as they like until they find a relationship that works for them. In formal, structured programmes that isn't so easy. Again, there have evolved some practical ground rules that avoid some of the worst problems:

- ☐ Avoid 'shotgun marriages' wherever possible. The least successful matches are typically those where the mentor and mentee feel they have been imposed upon each other. Next least successful are those where pairings are nominated by top management. If you cannot allow people some element of choice, at least make sure that participants understand how the matching process has been made. SmithKlineBeecham, before its recent merger with GlaxoWellcome, installed match-making software that included a variety of information about the mentee's learning needs, the mentor's experience and some general psychometric data, intended to avoid strong clashes of learning styles.

    The greatest level of buy-in from participants seems to come from giving the mentee a selection of three potential mentors, whom they can meet if they wish. It is very rare for anyone to ask for more than the original three. Making it clear that mentees will make their selection according to the degree of rapport they feel and the closeness of match with their learning need seems to overcome most of the potential problems of mentors feeling turned down.

☐ Equally, avoid giving people an unguided choice. Experience suggests that many people will select as a mentor someone whom they know well and get on with. Alternatively, they will seek a high-flyer on whose coat-tails they can hang. Neither is likely to lead to a successful mentoring relationship. Too much familiarity allows little grit in the oyster – the amount of learning potential is relatively low. Seeking a high-flyer starts the relationship off with a set of unhealthy expectations. Moreover, the high-flyer may be too preoccupied with his or her own career to give much time to someone else.

☐ Avoid too great a hierarchy or experience gap between mentor and mentee. Figure 8 illustrates the point.

*Figure 8*

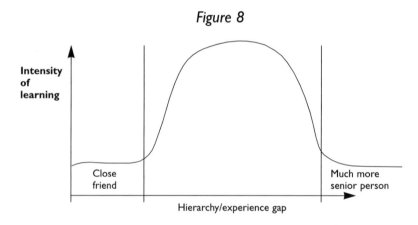

If the experience gap is too narrow, mentor and mentee will have little to talk about. If it is too great, the mentor's experience will be increasingly irrelevant to the mentee. Whereas once upon a time we could broadly say that there should not be more than two layers of hierarchy between mentor and mentee, organisation structures are now so complex and a single layer of management may hide such a wide variation in status, experience and ability that such a simple rule no longer suffices. It is up to the mentee and the programme co-ordinator to establish an appropriate learning distance.

An extension of the same principle is shown in Figure 9.

### Figure 9

In the top right corner, the relatively immature learner or the person lacking confidence will often feel more comfortable with someone who shares a similar functional background and per-haps common interests and views outside of work. At the other extreme, a highly self-confident, mature learner may welcome the challenge of learning with someone with whom they have very little in common. (A classic case here is the CEO of a local authority whose mentor is a highly educated Indian pharmacist in the same borough. The CEO uses the mentor as a sounding-board on issues that affect the sizeable local ethnic community; the pharmacist has a passionate interest in politics, although only as a passive observer.) Other people may select a mentor who is different enough to give the relationship some learning 'bite' but similar enough to make it easy to build and maintain rapport.

Although this approach seems rather mechanical, it does seem to be how well-informed HR professionals make their instinctive choices about who they should recommend to pair. It also helps in decisions about how close the mentor should be to the mentee in organisation terms. In many modern pro-grammes, the mentor's different perspective is a critical element of the relationship. At a large UK retailer, for example, mentees in the finance division were divided into two groups: those who needed to become more effective in their functional responsibil-ities, for whom a mentor from finance was provided, and those who were technically proficient but who needed greater commercial awareness, who were given mentors from sales, merchandising and marketing.

☐ Avoid entanglements between line and off-line relationships.

Most companies with mentoring programmes aimed at managers, for example, prefer to establish the relationship outside the normal working hierarchy. One reason for this is that there are times in the mentoring relationship when both sides need to back off. This is something much easier to do if there is a certain distance between them, either in hierarchical level or departmental function, or both. In addition, the boss – subordinate relationship, with all its entanglements of decisions on pay rises, disciplinary responsibilities and performance appraisal, may work against the openness and candour of the true mentoring relationship. The line manager may also not have a sufficiently wide experience of other job opportunities. Moreover, unless the line manager mentors all his or her direct reports – which would involve a very substantial time commitment – there is likely to be resentment from those people who are not mentored, while those who are become cast as favourites. This doesn't help build team unity!

☐ Ensure that mentors are committed to the programme.

A manager who is outstanding in his or her field may at first glance seem to be an ideal candidate for a mentor. It is just this sort of flair and expertise the company needs to pass on. However, if this manager's communication skills are extremely poor, or the manager resents being taken from his or her work because of mentorship obligations, he or she is unlikely to function well in the role. The company, the mentor and the mentee may all suffer in these circumstances.

Such a situation arose in one company where the programme co-ordinators attempted to assign mentors to mentees instead of allowing them to volunteer. They picked the most talented employee in research, who reluctantly agreed to act as a mentor. However, the mentee found his mentor was usually inaccessible and rarely spent time with him. The programme co-ordinators were reluctant to assign the mentee to another person for fear of offending his mentor. Trapped by the company politics, the mentee felt his career was being sacrificed to cover up the mistakes of senior management. Not surprisingly, he left to seek his career development elsewhere.

The moral of this story is clear. Companies should choose mentors who can not only communicate their skills well, but who are also actively committed to the programme. Every volunteer mentor is worth a dozen press-ganged ones. It is not necessary for the mentor to dazzle the mentee with superior knowledge and experience; he or she merely has to be able to encourage the mentee by sharing his or her own enthusiasm for the job. The mentor must be ready to invest time and effort into the relationship, so his or her interests will probably already lie in the areas of communication and interpersonal skills. The mentor must be ready to extend friendship to the mentee and be willing to let the relationship extend beyond the normal limits of a business relationship. The mentor should not participate in the programme unless he or she is willing to consider the relationship as a relatively long-term commitment.

☐ Allow for a 'no-fault divorce clause'. It is standard good practice now for mentors and mentees to be required to review the progress of the relationship after two or three meetings, with a view to assessing how suited they are to each other. If the conclusion is that they are not, the mentor can help the mentee think through what sort of mentor – if any – he or she needs at this time. We now have a small number of cases of relationships that have been dissolved in such a process but that have subsequently resumed – perhaps years later – when the mentee's circumstances and needs have changed.

## Summary

In this chapter we have explored some of the characteristics of the people who make the relationship work and some principles around the process of bringing them together. In the next chapter, we look at the structure of the mentoring programme and the requirements of its co-ordinator.

# 7 SETTING UP THE MENTORING PROGRAMME

Some form of spontaneous mentoring takes place in most organisations, whether acknowledged or not. A formalised programme helps harness it to the organisation's objectives. Properly managed, the programme can enhance the benefits to individuals from informal mentoring and minimise the problems that arise when the informal system bypasses talented employees.

There are usually four people involved in a mentoring programme. Together, they make up a mentoring quadrangle:

☐ the mentee
☐ the mentor
☐ the line manager
☐ the programme co-ordinator, who monitors the relationships and looks at resources for training opportunities.

*Figure 10*

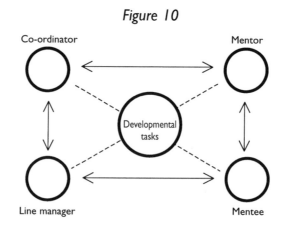

The clearer all four are about the objectives and effort required, the more successful the programme will be. All must be involved and consulted about career moves and developmental tasks that will take the mentee away from day-to-day work and responsibilities.

Each organisation has to draw up a mentoring programme that fits its particular company culture and answers the needs of its own employees. To ensure the success of the mentoring programme, a company must be prepared to be flexible in its approach and be willing to assess continuously and, if necessary, modify the methods it has implemented.

The starting-point, as with any major corporate programme, must be a clear statement of objectives against which progress may be measured. Typical objectives might be:

□ to establish a cadre of broadly trained generalist managers at or just below middle management
□ to speed and improve the induction of specific types of recruits and reduce wastage within the first year of their employment
□ to allow top management to assess the ability of both individual young managers and the rising generation of managers as a whole
□ to provide equal opportunities for disadvantaged groups of employees.

In each case, the personnel department can establish with top management a set of assessment criteria and a timetable for achieving specific levels of results.

Putting these objectives into practice requires a great deal of preparation. Usually at least six months to a year is needed to gain acceptance of the concept from the key people in the organisation, to establish objectives and measurements, to design supporting facilities, such as special training courses, and to begin the process of selecting participants.

Before setting up its mentoring programme, for example, the Burton Group's HR department decided to look at the following:

□ the internal set-up and relationships
□ support systems
□ timescales to be agreed
□ obtaining the managing director's commitment
□ determining how it would select mentors

☐ deciding how it would prepare mentoring workshops
☐ deciding how to match the mentor and mentee
☐ introducing the mentor and the mentee
☐ the line manager's role.

Throughout this process, the following principles are essential to bear in mind:

☐ ensure top management commitment
☐ adapt the programme to the company's development programme
☐ ensure commitment and participation from mentor/mentee groups
☐ ensure an acceptance of the time involved
☐ demystify the mentoring programme
☐ ensure confidentiality
☐ measure both processes and outcomes (see Chapter 8).

## Preparing the company for a mentoring programme

### Ensure top management commitment

Ensure that top management is committed to the programme. The top management team needs to supply decisive leadership to demonstrate to the rest of the company that it considers mentoring to be a legitimate and effective method of developing and improving staff potential. Top management must support the programme verbally and materially. It must promote mentoring within the company, through speeches, letters, memoranda and articles in the company newsletter. Articles in the public media can reinforce the message greatly, because employees often take greater note of information they read in independent newspapers and magazines than they do of the same information presented in official company publications. Senior management can also attend general meetings of groups of mentoring pairs. These strategies are especially necessary if general unease, confusion, or even suspicion about the programme exists in the company.

### Adapt the programme to the company's development programme

Try to fit the mentoring programme into the context of a wider framework of employee development and human resource

management, and explain this framework to employees. Problems are likely to arise if the programme exists in isolation. If it
seems that mentoring is the only form of career development in
the company, employees may easily assume that those chosen to
participate are destined automatically for senior management.
The company could be accused of having a promotion system
based solely on favouritism. The morale of those not on the programme would suffer appreciably. Those individuals who are on
the programme may be encouraged to believe that all their
chances of promotion lie in the mentoring relationship. As a
result, they may throw all their efforts into that area and neglect
other aspects of their work. To avoid these pitfalls, mentoring
should be seen as only one dimension of career development.

The company should also make sure mentees have other
opportunities to improve their skills beyond those arising within
the mentoring programme. They should have access to internal
or external workshops, self-development and distance-learning
materials, as well as career development classes. This is to
ensure that mentees can easily supplement their knowledge if
the mentor's coaching is too specialised or fails to be sufficiently
relevant and helpful. If the mentee is forced to rely solely on an
inefficient mentor, he or she can feel frustrated and limited by
the relationship. For people from disenfranchised groups and/or
minorities, the company may wish in addition to make available
some form of assertiveness training. At a recent round-table discussion in Washington (at the Linkage Coaching and Mentoring
Conference, July 2001), the point was made quite strongly by
some participants that in order to participate fully in mixed-
gender mentoring training, or in cross-gender mentoring relationships, many women benefited from help in learning how to
put their own views and perceptions more forcibly.

### Ensure commitment and participation

Ensure that participation is voluntary. Mentoring demands time
and effort so the essential ingredient is commitment. When a
company requests staff to volunteer to be mentors, it should
make sure that it emphasises how demanding the relationship
is. The programme co-ordinator should talk to all mentor applicants before making the final decision. If an assessment centre
approach is used to select mentees, consideration should be

given to designing an assessment centre for mentors, too.

Potential mentors should be informed of problems and challenges and what they should expect of the relationship. Some companies give all new mentors and mentees the chance to hear from existing mentors of the pitfalls and pleasures mentoring can bring. They also explore the mentee's view through the eyes of previous participants. The co-ordinator should also attempt to discover any ambivalence the mentor may feel about his or her commitment.

### Ensure support systems are in place

The most important of the support systems required are:

☐ clear information about the purpose of the programme and who is eligible for it

☐ some basic information about mentoring and how to apply for the programme – the Department for Employment and Education, for example, has an extensive website on its intranet

☐ a systematic, transparent system for matching mentors and mentees – the European Mentoring Centre can provide up-to-date information on software available

☐ a well-focused training programme for both mentor and mentee

☐ some form of mutual support mechanism, where mentors can meet from time to time to share experience and receive further advice (along the lines of supervision in counselling, although not necessarily so structured); at London Borough of Ealing, mentors meet in small groups with an experienced facilitator and mentor trainer who works with them and helps them learn from the issues they have encountered as mentors.

Some companies, such as Procter & Gamble, have supported diversity mentoring schemes with newsletters and discussion sheets aimed at stimulating dialogue between mentor and mentee. Other companies feel that most people will rapidly establish their own agenda.

### Ensure an acceptance of the time involved

Make sure everyone understands the amount of time commitment involved. As part of the preparation of the mentor, the mentee and the mentee's manager must be devoted to establishing just how much of each person's time will be taken up by the scheme. This time has to be planned for, regular meetings scheduled and a timetable established for any project work agreed.

Two key questions that must be asked are:

☐ How disruptive to the normal work of these people will the time commitment be?
☐ How valuable will this time and effort be in achieving the objective of developing the mentee?

Two useful ground rules help to put the time issue into perspective:

☐ If you meet less than once a quarter, you haven't got a relationship (it's just an acquaintance); if you meet much more than once a month, the mentor is probably doing the line manager's job.
☐ Ideally, meetings should last 60–90 minutes. Below this, it's difficult to address issues in real depth. Above two hours and you are probably going round the houses. It can be good practice to put an extra half hour into the diary to allow for those occasions when a really crucial issue comes to the surface towards the end of the scheduled time.

### Demystify the mentoring programme

Demystify the mentoring programme for those who are not involved. The methods and objectives of the programme should be explained clearly, setting out and emphasising the benefits to the organisation as a whole. If it is decided to establish only a small number of mentoring pairs as a pilot at the beginning of a programme, the organisation should explain to applicants not included that they will have an opportunity to reapply in the future.

### Ensure confidentiality

Confidentiality is essential if the mentee is to open up to the mentor to produce the kind of frank relationship necessary for success. BP Chemicals ensures that all exchanges are covered by a rule of confidentiality so that the mentee can speak to the mentor as a trusted friend. One mentor comments: 'The mentor should be completely aside from the line of work. It is important that total honesty and openness can be displayed, and often mentees feel wary if they do not have the distance they would like.'

Confidentiality in mentoring is rarely absolute. Leaving aside the issue of legal obligations (eg becoming an accessory after the fact), different organisations have different expectations of the level of confidentiality that can apply. At District Audit, the mentor is obliged to report any indication of financial misconduct, for example. At a City financial services company, top management has been careful to draw the distinction between privacy (being able to talk about issues in a relationship of trust) and confidentiality (the expectation that nothing said can be discussed outside the relationship without mutual agreement).

Clearly, the less confidence the mentee (let alone the mentor) has that what he or she says will remain between them alone, the more reluctant the mentee will be in speaking openly of his or her feelings and concerns. Said one mentee recently:

> My line manager and my mentor play golf together every Sunday. There are things I'd like to explore with the mentor, about how to tackle some of my manager's behaviours, but I'm never sure how much I dare say. If my manager thought I was criticising him behind his back, I'd have a real problem. As it is, twice now they have both made much the same suggestion to me about an issue I've brought up, which makes me suspicious that they have been discussing me.

Although issues of broken confidentiality are remarkably rare in mentoring, concerns over confidentiality remain one of the biggest limiting factors on relationships. Making the ground rules clear and trying, wherever possible, to avoid mentor and line manager being too close operationally or personally, are obvious practical measures to take.

Some of the engineering institutes have used mentoring for years as a means of assisting people on their route to chartered engineer. Most expected the mentor to carry out some form of assessment of the mentee, but this practice is gradually being dropped, not least because it introduced a dynamic into the relationship that made it difficult for the mentee to seek anything but technical advice – much of which was more readily available from other sources. To enrich the relationships and help build rounded professionals, the Institute of Electrical Engineers has largely divorced the measurement processes from the mentoring process.

## How to prepare the mentor and the mentee

It is essential to supply as much information as possible to the two most important participants of the programme – the mentor and the mentee – for both need to understand the purpose and objectives of the programme for the individual and for the company. Both also need to understand what is expected of them. The advantages of the relationship to both the mentor and the mentee should be particularly emphasised.

### The mentor

The most important aim in the preparatory stage of the programme is to motivate the mentor and help him or her see how he or she can contribute to the mentee's development.

#### Training

An organisation can run workshops for the mentor suggesting various methods of 'helping to learn'. A series of sessions might deal with:

- the purpose of the programme
- the benefits of the mentoring relationship
- something about mentoring
- the dynamic nature of the relationship, its stages and phases
- the core qualities and skills of an effective mentor
- practical tools and techniques for helping the mentee
- anticipating and forestalling possible problems
- adapting mentoring practices to particular settings.

It would also provide opportunities to put the skills into practice, through role play or through tackling real issues in a one-off mentoring environment.

These workshops could operate through brainstorming

sessions as well as role play and critique sessions so that mentors can assist each other to develop greater skills. The sessions would also encourage mentors to act as a support network for each other. Typically, in the UK, the mentor training workshops last one to two days and focus both on building awareness of the role and on raising awareness of key mentoring skills. In practice, however, many organisations now insist that initial training be carried out in much shorter periods. This poses a real challenge for the trainer, who must not only ensure that mentors emerge from less than half a day's training with enough understanding and confidence to try being a mentor, but must also find innovative ways of encouraging them to come back to review their progress. One current programme in the City is building in time for an external coach to sit in on mentoring sessions and provide mentors with a one-to-one briefing on their approach.

British American Tobacco (BAT) adopted a very flexible approach when it designed its international graduate mentoring programme. First, it linked together mentoring and coaching as parallel programmes, training managers in both skills, and training mentees in what to expect from the immediate line manager in the form of coaching and from the off-line mentor. The programmes were encapsulated in ring binders, available to all workshop participants. To customise the programme to the varying requirements of its subsidiaries around the world, the training manuals were designed to be recast as needed into one-day, one-and-a-half-day and two-day versions. The case studies were also replaceable, as needed, with local examples more suited to the national culture. Trainers from around the world were trained as facilitators with authority to adapt the materials to local circumstances. (Some had participated in the original design, as well, to make sure it met a wide range of needs.)

Is it possible to do without training at all? Practical experience suggests this usually results in a high proportion of failed relationships and severe damage to the concept of mentoring within the organisation. A rough-and-ready rule of thumb is that programmes introduced without any training, or with a minimalist briefing, rarely result in more than one in three relationships delivering any significant benefits to the participants. The fact that any relationships work at all seems to relate to the previous experience of mentoring by the people concerned and to the innate and instinctive competence some people have in the mentoring role. Training the mentor can double the success rate to six out of 10; training mentor and mentee, plus ensuring that the line managers also understand the purpose of the scheme and its benefits to them, pushes the success rate to over 90 per cent.

*Examine risks*

Organisations can help the mentor to examine frankly the potential risks involved in being a mentor. Programme co-ordinators should make it clear to the mentor and the company in general that the relationship is not guaranteed to be successful and that a failed pairing will not reflect badly on the mentor. Indeed, having the self-confidence to wind down a relationship that is not going anywhere should be seen as a sign of the mentor's developmental competence.

*Cross-gender relationships*

Alert 'cross-gender' mentors to the potential problems. The discovery that rumour and sexual innuendo exists about a mentoring couple can decisively restrict or even destroy the relationship. If the two parties are forewarned, they can cope with the external pressures better or adopt strategies to avoid giving encouragement to rumour.

*Networking*

Introduce the mentor to other managers who have experience in mentoring and who can discuss the various stages of the relationship and the challenges and difficulties that are likely to arise. Organisations can also appoint a senior or 'super' mentor to counsel and guide the less experienced mentor.

*Online training*

If appropriate, the company can provide training on demand using e-learning. There is a growing variety of resources here and at least one UK company is introducing its own e-learning programme in mentoring independently.

*Mentoring certificate*

For some people, the opportunity to obtain a certificate is attractive. The National Standards in Mentoring document issued in 2000 after piloting with 300 organisations, from companies to schools, is intended to eventually form the basis of a mentoring NVQ, and other formal qualifications are starting to appear. Great care needs to be exercised in determining the value and validity of some of these diplomas and certificates, some of which seem to have only marginal relevance to mentoring.

## The mentee

If the mentee is to take appropriate responsibility for the relationship, he or she needs to understand:

☐ what the organisation expects from the programme
☐ what can realistically be expected of the mentor
☐ what the mentor should expect of him or her
☐ what he or she can do to make the relationship deliver positive outcomes for both parties.

In most of the programmes that I have worked on over the past five years, the style of the mentee training depends very much on the maturity of the target audience. Young people in community schemes, ex-offenders and recent graduate recruits tend to be trained in a peer group. People at more senior level, or who are generally more experienced, tend to be included in a mixed group with mentors. The rationale behind this is first that mentor and mentee will manage the relationship better if they appreciate how it appears from the other side, and second that mentors can improve their skills if they also become mentees, and mentees if they in turn act as mentors. Incorporating role swaps into the training encourages insight into appropriate behaviours and helps build the kind of openness under which the relationship will flourish. Although it does sometimes happen that an intended mentoring pair train together, training usually occurs before matching takes place – so this provides another opportunity for the mentee to vet some potential mentors.

An additional element I have introduced into many mentee training workshops is a more intensive session on building and using networks. The more adept the mentee becomes at using networking, the more helpful the mentor can be. A good starting-point for developing learning nets is the peer group, which may have all the knowledge the graduate mentee needs to gain introductions to areas of the business he or she would like to know about. Similarly, some skills in career self-management come in very useful.

At a more senior level, the scheme co-ordinator may spend time helping mentees think through the nature of the transition they would like to make and how exactly they think a mentor can help. This both assists in the selection phase and ensures that the relationship can get started with a relatively clear sense of purpose.

## Getting started

Although a handful of companies start the whole process with a meeting at which the line manager or the scheme co-ordinator facilitates, in general this is perceived to be unnecessarily intrusive. Instead, mentor and mentee are usually encouraged to meet at a mutually convenient and not too formal place to work out on their own how they want to run their relationship. However, the primary objective of the first meeting is to get to know each other and build the rapport they will need to make the relationship work.

At this or the next meeting, the mentee should also be prepared to share with the mentor any information he or she has that is relevant to issues he or she wants to work on – for example, performance appraisals, assessment centre results or the outcomes of psychometric tests undertaken. I often ask my mentees to record once a week or so the three things that have most pleased and most frustrated them. Then either we examine the list together, to look for patterns, or the mentees extract their own meaning from the list before we meet. In this way, the dialogue becomes grounded in actual, recent experience rather than hypotheticals. Long-term developmental goals can be illuminated through examining more recent successes and failures.

## The role of the line manager v that of the mentor

To avoid clashes between mentor and line manager, or worse, deliberate manipulation of them by the mentee, it is important that line manager and mentor are clear about where the boundaries of their responsibility towards the mentee lie. Table 3 attempts to distinguish between the responsibilities and indicate where the responsibility is shared. Some organisations may wish to move the responsibilities around to suit their specific circumstances – no problem, as long as line managers and mentors are clear where they stand.

## Testing the programme

Start in a modest way to make sure that the initial effort is well designed and fulfils its objectives. Once a trial programme, involving say 5–20 mentoring pairs, has been successfully established, the company can decide to be more ambitious and expand its size and timescale. In this way the organisation can avoid most of the disillusionment and backlash that can come when a full-blown programme fails to live up to its objectives.

### *Table 3* DEVELOPMENT ROLES OF LINE MANAGER AND MENTOR

| Line manager | Shared | Mentor |
|---|---|---|
| Appraise performance | Encourage learner, motivate to learn | Help learner develop insights into causes of poor performance |
| Agree developmental goals within learner's current job | Shape goals beyond current job | Help learner manage the integration of job, career and personal goals |
| Help learner build relationships within the team | Help learner build relationships outside the team | Help learner build relationships with line manager |
| Find opportunities to stretch learner's performance | Find opportunities to stretch learner's thinking | Challenge learner's thinking and assumptions |
| Give constructive feedback through observation | Help learner develop skills of intrinsic observation | Help learner accept and manage feedback constructively |
| Role model for task fulfilment and growth | Role model of general behaviour | Role model for personal achievement and growth |

## The role of the training department

Just how far the training department does and should become involved varies from organisation to organisation. At British Gas, for example, four-way communication between the different points of the mentoring quadrangle is emphasised, although, according to one of its recruitment and development reports:

> Line managers are expected to liaise with mentors, rather than with the training department, although the training department does provide a 'safety net' for mentoring relationships that go wrong.
>
> A major role of the training department is communication. The department has recently published guidelines, for example, making clear in advance to mentors and line managers the kind of time commitment graduates need to give to the graduate programme and specific development projects. The company's electronic mail network allows the training department to communicate frequently with both mentors and graduates.

At the opposite extreme, other companies take a more relaxed approach, where the training department delivers initial training, then steps back and becomes involved only for troubleshooting purposes.

There is, of course, no right answer, except the one that works in the particular organisation. It *is* important, however, that the training department makes sure that it and everyone else involved clearly understands the role it intends to play.

## Summary

To be really successful, a mentoring programme must obtain acceptance and commitment from participants and non-participants alike. The scheme should have empathetic, carefully selected and trained mentors, mentees who understand how to make the most of opportunities, and clear goals accepted by all. A great deal of effort is therefore needed to prepare employees at all levels for the introduction of the programme, ensuring that everyone knows what is happening, why and how the scheme will work. Particular attention should be given to the mentoring pairs, the mentee's boss and the mentee's peers. Starting small with a modest experiment helps take some of the bugs out of the system before it is applied generally throughout the organisation.

# 8 RUNNING THE MENTORING PROGRAMME

The relationship should develop swiftly and smoothly if both mentor and mentee have been well matched and well prepared. The phases the relationship typically goes through are examined in the next chapter. In this short section we look at how to make sure that the mentoring pair make the most of the opportunity given them.

By the time the mentor and mentee hold their first formal meeting under the mentoring programme, both should have a clear idea of the objectives of the relationship. These may be relatively vague at this stage, not least because the programme is intended to help the mentee refine and develop his or her career objectives. However, it should at least start with some form of assessment of the mentee's strengths and weaknesses, the nature of the transition he or she would like to make, and what the longer-term ambitions are. It will also, of course, take into account the general programme objectives, which both parties should understand clearly.

Typical starting objectives might include the following:

□ Introduce the mentee to other, parallel functions or departments whose work he or she will need to understand to progress or that may open his or her eyes to potential sideways moves.

□ Help the mentee break down a seemingly impossible or far-fetched goal into a series of more tangible tasks that he or she can begin to address. Having a more or less detailed route-map of the experience, skills and competencies he or she needs to gather, the mentee can enter onto a self-development or career management path with greater confidence and commitment.

□ Help the mentee think through how to raise his or her visibility where it matters.

- Help the mentee establish the informal networks he or she needs to be effective in the organisation.
- Act as a sounding-board in helping the mentee work out how to manage difficult relationships with working colleagues.
- Help the mentee think through how to apply in practice what he or she is learning through theoretical study.
- Gain a real understanding of the career choices that face the mentee and the implications of each choice.

Some organisations prefer to set out objectives in terms of process rather than outcomes. For example, a large UK chemical company sets out the following responsibilities at the beginning of a mentoring relationship:

- Meet the mentee once a month for an hour by timetabling formally in advance.
- Ensure that the mentee maintains a brief diary of daily events to form the basis for the monthly discussion.
- Develop a personal relationship with the mentee.
- Maintain the relationship for two years.

The objectives will be defined and adopted as the relationship develops and as the mentee's needs change. It is also expected that the two people start off with the same understanding of the ground rules of the relationship. In particular, there have to be clear rules of behaviour.

Another common guideline is: 'The mentor will only communicate his or her knowledge of the mentee to other parties with the mentee's consent.'

A more detailed and generic code of practice for the mentoring relationship is that designed for the National Standards and is reproduced in the box below. Some organisations provide a general set of core rules for all mentoring relationships; others leave it to the individuals to decide. Whichever route they choose, the aim is to help the mentee stand on his or her own feet, not to make him or her dependent.

---

### AN ETHICAL CODE OF PRACTICE FOR MENTORING

- ☐ The mentor's role is to respond to the mentee's developmental needs and agenda; it is not to impose his or her own agenda.

- ☐ Mentors must work within the current agreement with the mentee about confidentiality that is appropriate within the context.

- ☐ The mentor will not intrude into areas the mentee wishes to keep private until invited to do so. However, he or she should help the mentee recognise how other issues may relate to those areas.

- ☐ Mentor and mentee should aim to be open and truthful with each other and themselves about the relationship itself.

- ☐ The mentoring relationship must not be exploitative in any way, nor can it be open to misinterpretation.

- ☐ Mentors need to be aware of the limits of their own competence and operate within these limits.

- ☐ Mentors have a responsibility to develop their own competence in the practice of mentoring.

- ☐ The mentee must accept increasing responsibility for managing the relationship; the mentor should empower them to do so and must generally promote the mentee's autonomy.

- ☐ Mentor and mentee should respect each other's time and other responsibilities, ensuring that they do not impose beyond what is reasonable.

- ☐ Mentor and mentee share responsibility for the smooth winding down of the relationship when it has achieved its purpose – they must both avoid creating dependency.

- ☐ Either party may dissolve the relationship. However, both mentor and mentee have a responsibility for discussing the matter together as part of mutual learning.

- ☐ The mentee should be aware of his or her rights and any complaints procedures.

- ☐ Mentors must be aware of any current law and work within the law.

- ☐ Mentor and mentee must be aware that all records are subject to statutory regulations under the Data Protection Act 1998.

---

## Measuring and monitoring the programme

The company also needs some system of feedback and evaluation in order to know whether mentoring is functioning efficiently and successfully. For example, one large UK manufacturing company holds a graduate workshop at least once a year so graduate mentees can get together and produce a report recommending changes in the system.

In fact, there are three main reasons for measuring:

☐ to troubleshoot individual relationships

☐ to provide information for quality improvement of the mentoring programme

☐ to demonstrate to top management that the investment in mentoring has been worthwhile.

BP Chemicals is unusual in that it audits its scheme annually, both to improve the scheme and to demonstrate that the company takes mentoring seriously. The audit shows mentoring works best when:

☐ graduates meet their mentors shortly after arriving on site

☐ early meetings are regular and the mentors appear purposeful and confident

☐ the relationship feels 'real'

☐ the mentor and mentee are on the same site but in different parts of the company

☐ both mentor and mentee start with the premise that mentoring is 'good'

☐ the mentor is not a line manager to the mentee

☐ graduates use diary notes to discuss what they have been doing since the last meeting.

One of the paradoxes of formal mentoring programmes is that the essence of the relationship is its *informality* – the ability to discuss in private a wide range of issues that will help the mentee cope with and learn from issues he or she encounters, putting aside any power or status differences that might operate outside the relationship. So the idea of measurement and review is, on the face of it, to some extent at odds with the need to retain a high degree of informality and ad hoc responsiveness.

In practice, a certain amount of measurement provides the foundation on which the informal relationship can grow most healthily. It allows:

☐ scheme co-ordinators to recognise where additional support is needed and to improve the operation of the scheme – not least the training

☐ mentors and mentees to work together to build the relationship, understanding more clearly what each can and does bring to the discussions.

Where attempts to measure mentoring become unacceptable, they usually involve:

☐ an attempt to assess and report upon mentees' performance to a third party

☐ a link between the mentor's opinion and a specific reward for the mentee (a promotion or a diploma, for example) – here the role has become more that of a tutor

☐ disclosure of the content of discussions.

In such circumstances, measurement is likely to make the mentee – and sometimes the mentor – less open, less willing to admit weaknesses and less trusting, hence limiting the potential of the relationship to deliver high quantity and quality of learning.

By contrast effective measurement in mentoring is:

☐ relatively unobtrusive

☐ valued by all parties as helpful

☐ timely

☐ straightforward and easy to apply.

## The measurement matrix

Mentoring measurements fall into four categories, illustrated in Figure 11:

☐ Relationship processes – what happens in the relationship; for example, how often does the pair meet? Have they developed sufficient trust? Is there a clear sense of direction to the relationship? Does the mentor or the mentee have concerns about their own or the other person's contribution to the relationship?

☐ Programme processes – for example, how many people attended training? How effective was the training? In some cases, programme processes will also include data derived from adding together measurements from individual relationships, to gain a broad picture of what is going well and less well.

☐ Relationship outcomes – have mentor and mentee met the goals they set? (Some adjustment may be needed for legitimate changes in goals as circumstances evolve.)

☐ Programme outcomes – have we, for example, increased retention of key staff, or raised the competence of the mentees in critical areas?

Measuring all four gives you a balanced view of the mentoring programme and allows the scheme co-ordinator to intervene, with sensitivity, where needed.

*Figure 11*

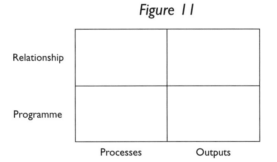

Table 4 shows the actual measures used by SmithKline-Beecham's finance division. The total number of measures was kept to a maximum of 10, covering the full spectrum of hard and soft measures, process and output and relationship and programme measures.

## What should be reviewed when?

*At the programme planning stage*

There is a need at both programme and relationship level for a clear purpose up front and a clear idea of what behaviours are expected from both mentors and mentees. It is good practice to involve potential participants and other interested parties (eg line managers, top management) to agree measurements at the beginning. At the very least this discussion will establish the extent to which measurements can be 'soft' (qualitative) or 'hard' (quantitative).

*Table 4*

| Corporate process | Corporate outcome/goals |
|---|---|
| 1  How often: at least 5 meetings<br>2  What phase: set direction + working<br>   towards targets<br>3  People are networking more | 1  Mentee is asking for development<br>   opportunities<br>2  Has a plan/action around raising<br>   personal profile |
| **Relationship process** | **Relationship outcomes** |
| 1  Do we trust each other/work together<br>   well?<br>2  Are we dealing with real issues?<br>3  Do I enjoy it? | 1  Has significant learning taken place?<br>2  Have you gained in competence in<br>   an area you wanted to work on? |

Many organisations now begin the programme with a short research project to establish likely barriers and drivers to mentoring.

*In selecting/training mentors and mentees*

Mentors and mentees can benefit from greater self-awareness of their strengths and weaknesses as developers of others. Mentees often need to have some ideas about the areas of interpersonal behaviour they can work on with the mentor.

*After the first few meetings*

This is the opportunity for mentor and mentee to review whether the relationship is going to work. Key questions here include:

☐ Have we established strong rapport and trust, sufficient to work together?

☐ Does the mentee perceive the mentor's input as relevant and stimulating?

☐ If not, what sort of person does the mentee need to work with?

The scheme co-ordinator will want by this point to know whether people are meeting and whether they have discussed the future of the relationship.

*As the relationship progresses*

The scheme co-ordinator will want at the minimum to know what further support is needed, if any, in the form of further, more focused skills training, or general encouragement to participants. Good practice typically involves a short survey of participants, followed by a review session during which some ad hoc training can be provided.

*At the end of the relationship*

Assuming the relationship achieves its objectives and winds down, it is useful for both parties to review the following:

- □ What did we expect to achieve?
- □ What did we actually achieve?
- □ What else did we learn on the way?
- □ How will we use what we have learnt in future developmental relationships?

*At the end of the programme*

Assuming the programme assigns an end to the formal mentoring relationship (many relationships will, of course, continue informally thereafter), the outcomes can be measured against the original goals.

## The mentoring contract

The notion of a mentoring contract is widespread and poses a similar conundrum to measurement. To what extent should we risk bureaucratising an essentially informal process? Some clarity is essential, but how much, and does a written document contribute greatly to clarity anyway?

There is no straightforward answer, not least because it depends on circumstance. In an experiment some years ago within the National Health Service, I provided 100 pairs of mentors and mentees with detailed discussion guides, formal contracts to sign and extensive background notes. I then invited them to use these religiously, to scan them and put them aside, or to ignore them altogether. When we reviewed the results, it became clear that only 20 per cent had completed the contracts, while the others had roughly half and half scanned or ditched them. The success rate of the relationships did not seem to be affected by their choice. From this, I conclude, it should be left to the mentee and mentor to decide how they approach the issue of contracting.

What does seem to be essential is that both sides discuss the relationship objectives, their expectations of each other and how they will manage the relationship. The following checklist seems to provide a basic set of questions most people can relate to in discussing these issues.

### *Mentoring ground rules*

1   a) Are we clear about each other's expectations of:
   - ☐ each other?
   - ☐ the mentoring relationship?
   - ☐ what we hope to learn from each other?
   b) How closely do our expectations match?
   c) How directive or non-directive should the mentor be in each meeting?

2   a) What are the core topics we want to discuss?
   b) What, if any, are the limits to the scope of discussion (ie what we talk about)?

3   Who will take primary responsibility – ie the mentor, the mentee or both together – for:
   - ☐ deciding how often to meet?
   - ☐ setting the agenda for meetings?
   - ☐ ensuring that meetings take place?
   - ☐ organising where to meet, and for how long?
   - ☐ defining learning goals?
   - ☐ initiating reviews of progress?

4   How formal or informal do we want our meetings to be?

5   To what extent is the mentor prepared to allow the mentee to:
   - ☐ use his or her authority?
   - ☐ use his or her networks?
   - ☐ take up time between meetings?

6   Are we agreed that openness and trust are essential? How will we ensure they happen?

7   Are we *both willing* to give honest and timely feedback (eg to be a critical friend)?

8   a) What, if any, are the limits to the confidentiality of this relationship?

　　　b) What are we prepared to tell others:
　　　　□  about the relationship?
　　　　□  about our discussions?
　　　c) Who shall we tell, and how?
　9　What responsibilities do we owe to others as a result of this relationship (eg to line managers, peers, the programme co-ordinator)?
　10　a) How do we ensure the mentee's line manager is suppor-tive?
　　　b) Is there a clear distinction between the roles of mentor and line manager?
　　　c) If there are overlaps, how will these be managed?
　11　When and how shall we check this relationship is 'right' for both of us?

## The role of the mentoring co-ordinator

The task of the mentoring co-ordinator can be quite formidable. He or she is the formal link between participants and top man-agement, the primary source of troubleshooting for relation-ships in difficulty and the person responsible for all the support mechanisms. Key activities include:

□  managing the publicity for the scheme and the recruitment of mentors and mentees
□  arranging initial training and follow-up
□  maintaining the website, where there is one
□  administering the matching process and any reassignments that are needed
□  ensuring that measurement and review processes take place when they are supposed to
□  managing the budgets and quality control processes
□  being the public face of the programme to audiences inside and outside the organisation.

One of the most common reasons mentoring programmes falter is that there is no one with the assigned time or priorities to devote to these activities. It is therefore imperative that before the company embarks on a major expansion of mentoring, it ensures there is sufficient management resource to support it. A rough calculation is that it requires one full day a week of an HR professional's time for every 20 mentoring pairs. Some companies with large graduate mentoring programmes ease the burden by assigning second-year graduate recruits to the HR department to absorb the bulk of the administrative burden. This is a prized assignment, as the graduate gets to know a very large slice of the organisation in the year or so he or she is attached to the project.

## Summary

The mentoring programme needs considerable maintenance; it cannot be left to its own devices. Monitoring of progress versus regularly reviewed objectives is essential to ensure that mentee, mentor and company all benefit from the scheme.

# 9 PHASES OF THE MENTORING RELATIONSHIP

In an experiment with several hundred HR professionals a few years ago, I asked people who they found to be their most frequent and most intensive sources of learning at work. The results, which have since been replicated with other groups of employees in a variety of circumstances, were stark – the most frequent learning came from peers, the most intensive from mentors. Line managers scored near the bottom of the pile on both criteria.

The relationship with the mentor influences the career and personal development of a young employee. In the early stages of his or her career the young employee's identity, career aspirations and business relationships are forming. The junior must learn new technical, political and interpersonal skills. Throughout this process, the mentor relationship is often the most important vehicle for stimulating and assisting his or her development. The mentor:

- offers friendship
- acts as a role model
- accepts and confirms the mentee's notions about his or her own identity
- provides support and encouragement
- gives confidence and a feeling of competence.

The mentor also finds that a relationship with a younger employee answers certain of his or her own psychological needs. The mid-career stage can be difficult for many managers and executives as they find there is little chance of any further growth or advancement. The mentor's career may be in danger of stagnation if he or she feels locked into a pattern of repetition and uniformity. Entering a mentoring relationship at that stage of the mentor's career provides refreshing new challenges.

Mentors can redirect their energies into a stimulating and creative role.

Mentoring demands a flexible and individual approach rather than applying habitual, well-used formulae. As a result, the mentor finds new self-respect as he or she recognises he or she has valuable experiences and knowledge to pass on to the mentee.

A major study into the nature of the mentoring process was conducted in the early 1980s by Katherine Kram (1983), then Assistant Professor of Organizational Behaviour at Boston University's School of Management. Kram attempted to discover the significance of the relationship for the mentor and the mentee and how mentoring influenced each party's career and self-development. She also tried to establish whether mentoring relationships share any similar characteristics.

Kram conducted her survey in a public utility company of 15,000 employees in the north-east region of the USA. She studied 18 mentoring pairs using in-depth interviews. The young mentees' ages ranged between 26 and 34, while the mentors' ages ranged between 39 and 63. The relationships varied considerably in duration, but Kram found that they were on average about five years long. Each relationship generally progressed through four distinct stages. In the remainder of this chapter we explore each of those phases – initiation (the start), the middle period, dissolving the relationship and restarting – alongside the slightly different evolution observed in developmental mentoring. Table 5 outlines these differences.

Kram's study was based on sponsorship mentoring and a definition that included both off-line and boss-subordinate relationships, so its general applicability to developmental mentoring is suspect. The phases she identifies ring broadly true, however, even if the conclusions drawn are not the same.

## The start of the relationship

During the first six months to a year of a successful mentoring relationship, says Kram, the young mentee may well hold an unrealistically ideal picture of the mentor. He or she frequently sees the mentor as an extremely competent figure who gives support and guidance. In these circumstances the mentee identifies strongly with the mentor and draws emotional support

### Table 5  THE PHASES OF RELATIONSHIP DEVELOPMENT: A COMPARISON OF US AND EUROPEAN APPROACHES

| Kram: US sponsoring mentoring | European (developmental) mentoring |
| --- | --- |
| Starting: suspicion evolves into trust and mutual respect | Rapport-building – getting to know each other |
| | Direction-setting – developing a sense of relationship purpose |
| | **6 months** |
| | Progress-making – high mutual learning |
| **12 months** | |
| Middle period – mentor uses influence to help mentee advance | |
| | **24 months** |
| Working towards setting personal and career goals | |
| | Winding down – celebrating success, moving on to new sources of learning |
| **36 months** | |
| Dissolving the relationship | **30 months** |
| | Continuing informally, infrequently as a sounding-board |
| Indeterminate | |
| Restarting the relationship – coming to terms with a different status | |

from the relationship. The young manager feels he or she is cared for by someone of great importance within the organisation.

The opposite, of course, may also occasionally be the case. A mentee may begin the relationship with a great deal of suspicion and an image of the more senior manager as a 'played-out timeserver'. How well the mentoring relationship works here will depend on whether the mentor wins the mentee's respect as the nature of the job he or she does and the difficulty of the decisions he or she takes become clearer.

For the mentor, the relationship with the mentee can also be highly rewarding during this period. The mentor is drawn to the mentee because of his or her potential and willingness to learn, seeing in the mentee someone to whom his or her own values and perspectives can be passed. In a successful relationship, mentors also derive satisfaction from recognising how they can speed the mentee's growth by supplying advice and support. Many mentors also comment on the sense of pride they have in seeing their mentees progress. Both mentor and mentee develop positive expectations of each other. By the end of the first year they have gained sufficient confidence in each other and in the relationship to set in motion more substantial arrangements for learning.

Observation of European mentoring relationships presents a somewhat different picture. For a start, the initiation phase seems to have two components – rapport-building and direction-setting. During rapport-building, the mentor and mentee test the water – can they work together easily? Deep friendship is not required, simply sufficient mutual respect, goodwill and relevance of experience to begin the journey.

Learning how to work together is a process of sharing that will gradually increase in intimacy as trust grows and positive experience of achieving useful insight accumulates. The mentor needs to exercise considerable skill at putting the mentee at ease, encouraging him or her to open up.

Direction-setting involves developing a consensus about the outcomes the mentee desires and some practical ideas about how to get there. The mentor needs considerable skills in helping the mentee clarify personal goals, build commitment to them and develop a practical and, if appropriate, opportunistic plan to achieve the relationship goals. The mentor may also be quite open about his or her own learning goals from the relationship – which in turn helps to reinforce the building of rapport.

### A checklist for the first meeting

1  Where shall we meet and for how long?
   PROP – (Professional, Relaxed, Open, Purposeful) for both parties
2  What do we want/need to know about each other?

*Social*
- ☐ career history
- ☐ domestic circumstances
- ☐ interests outside work

*Career ambition*
- ☐ what you enjoy/dislike about working in this industry
- ☐ where you want to be in five years' time
- ☐ greatest achievements/failures
- ☐ what your picture of success is
- ☐ how clear the mentee's career goals are

*Development goals*
- ☐ what the mentee wants to improve in
- ☐ for the current job
- ☐ in preparation for future jobs
- ☐ where the mentee would most value guidance/advice/a sounding-board

3 What will make this a satisfying and useful relationship for both of us?

4 What expectations do we have of each other (ground rules and verbal contract)?

5 What are our priorities?

6 How often and where shall we meet?

7 Do we want to set an agenda for our next meeting?

8 Are there any issues we should get to work on now?

## The middle period

Kram's middle period lasts for two to five years and is regarded as the most rewarding for the two parties. The relationship is cultivated as the mentor coaches and promotes his or her mentee. The friendship between the two strengthens as a high degree of trust and intimacy builds up between the mentor and mentee.

The mentor's ability to coach the mentee and clarify his or her sense of purpose and identity helps to improve the mentee's sense of self-worth. In sponsoring mentoring, the mentor provides the mentee with work opportunities that help to develop his or her managerial skills and confirm and reinforce the mentee's sense of competence and ability. The mentee understands the business scenario better and knows how better to control the work environment.

One mentee commented:

> I was very under-confident when I joined this company. I was newly divorced and I had not worked for quite some time. I was wholly intimidated by the business world. My mentor encouraged me to perform beyond my job description. She would criticise my performance, explain my mistakes and advise me on how to perform better. Above all she gave me confidence. She would say 'I know that you have the ability to do it, and I know that you *will* do it.' Her encouragement and faith in me was a great support and incentive.

It is at this stage that the mentor gains the most satisfaction from the knowledge that he or she has had an important effect on the mentee's development. One mentor tries to describe the pride he feels when he sees his mentee perform well and receive recognition from the company:

> The satisfaction I receive is similar to parental pride. You have put faith in that person and helped them develop. When they succeed, you feel it has all been worthwhile and you remember that you were instrumental in helping them to do so.

Mentors also receive technical and psychological help and support from their mentees. The mentee now has the skill to help his or her mentor as well as the ability to recognise the needs of the more senior manager. The mentor has a renewed sense of his or her own influence and power as he or she opens doors in the organisation for the mentee. The mentor also feels he or she is passing something to the company that will have lasting value. Through the mentee the sponsoring mentor can express his or her own perspectives and values.

In Kram's scenario, it often takes until this point for the mentor and the mentee to have agreed upon a set of development goals or even a career path, involving at least one and usually several clearly defined promotional or horizontal moves.

Discussions between the mentor and mentee now centre less on defining objectives than on strategies and tactics to achieve them. Project work that the line manager mentor sets his or her mentee is aimed both at developing skills and at assessing how well they have been absorbed. The two people meet regularly to review progress in each area where they have agreed improvement is necessary to qualify for the next career step. The mentor directs the mentee towards additional sources of learning and challenges him or her to prove the successes claimed.

Again the picture that emerges from developmental mentoring is different in a number of ways. For a start, the time horizon is often much shorter – many developmental mentoring relationships are well into the middle (or the progress-making) period after six months or so. Second, the mentor has no role in the projects or tasks the mentee undertakes, other than as a sounding-board. Third, the developmental mentoring relationship at this stage is characterised by a much deeper level of challenge, probing and analysis.

Fourth, the mentee begins to rely much more on his or her own judgement, and is less likely to seek the mentor's approval. Finally, the mentor often learns as much or more from their dialogue as do the mentees.

This highly fulfilling phase of the relationship often settles down to a routine where the pair are sufficiently familiar and comfortable with the process to explore more and more 'difficult' issues. Sensitive areas, which the mentee has avoided, now become admissible and may provide the deepest and most transforming issues for discussion.

Throughout this whole progress-making phase, the effective mentor demonstrates a remarkably consistent skill set – consistent, that is, with every other effective mentor. Figure 12 is based on observation of numerous mentors, ranging from the very effective to the very ineffective.

The most effective mentors, even those who are strongly activist and/or task-oriented, always start the process by re-establishing rapport. For a few minutes they engage in the normal social trivialities that help people relax in each other's company. Then they ask the mentee to explain briefly what issues he or she would like to explore. One of my favourite questions to executive mentees is, 'What's keeping you awake at night this week?'

Ineffective mentors listen briefly to the mentee's account and immediately relate the issue to their own experience, when they perceive it to be relevant. They tell the mentee what happened to them, how they tackled the issue, and what lessons they

*Figure 12* **THE MENTORING MEETING**

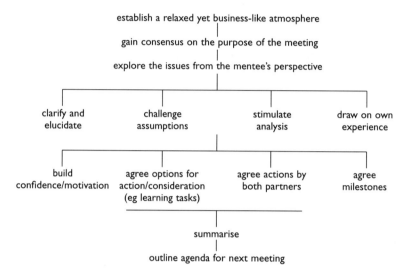

learned. As a result, they frequently end up advising on the presented issue, missing deeper, more important issues. Effective mentors hold fire. First, they ask for more facts and feelings – what exactly happened? How did you feel about it? Is this a one-off recurrence? Next, they challenge the assumptions behind the mentee's account – for example, what would an unbiased third party have thought if they were observing?

The responses to this probing, and the different perspectives generated, allow mentor and mentee to analyse the situation in some form of conceptual framework. For example, 'Let's look at how your behaviour might be influencing your colleagues and vice versa.' Finally, in this first half of the mentoring session, the mentor may draw upon his or her own experience to introduce additional considerations.

Having understood the issues better, mentor and mentee can concentrate on developing pragmatic solutions. Before launching into problem-solving mode, however, the mentor ensures that the mentee is in a sufficiently positive frame of mind – that he or she has the confidence to consider alternative approaches and the commitment to making a change happen. Through a variety of techniques, the mentor helps the mentee catalogue possible ways forward and assess them against the mentee's own values criteria. Having selected one or two to pursue, the pair agree who will do what in dealing with the issue. Ineffective mentors sometimes tend to take on extensive responsibilities; effective ones limit their role to tasks such as seeking out an article or report, or making an introduction. The effective mentor also presses the mentee to set mental deadlines by which he or she expects to have tackled at least the initial stages of the plan.

One final task remains – summarising what has been discussed. Ineffective mentors rush straight in and summarise for the mentee. In doing so, they both miss the chance to check there is a common understanding and take responsibility for the issue at least partially back onto their own shoulders. Effective mentors ensure that the mentee summarises and retains ownership of the issue throughout, including whether to bring the matter back to the agenda next time they meet.

## Dissolving the relationship

In Kram's model, after two to five years the mentoring relationship begins to draw apart. The mentor and the mentee are affected by organisational changes. The mentee has advanced sufficiently to be experiencing new independence and autonomy. The mentor relationship becomes less essential as the mentee's challenges change.

Mentees may respond differently when the relationship declines according to how prepared they are for the separation. If a change in career position occurs before the mentee feels ready to operate independently of the mentor, he or she will experience a time of uncertainty and anxiety. The mentee will miss the psychological support of the mentor and be aware that he or she no longer has a 'safety net' to fall upon if he or she makes a wrong decision. The unprepared mentee can also feel abandoned and betrayed and lose confidence.

One young British mentee found her first year apart from her mentor a very difficult time emotionally. A period of redefinition was necessary as she had to demonstrate to the rest of the organisation that she was able to operate independently without her mentor: 'I had to prove to myself and the rest of the company that it was my ability which got me my new job and not my mentor's influence. I had to show I could stand alone. I think the whole process helped me to mature. Now if I have any difficulties I rely on myself.'

If the mentee is fully prepared for separation from the mentor, he or she enjoys this new-found freedom and independence. It is a little like driving the car home after having passed the driving test.

Most mentors accept that their mentees must move away from them and become psychologically more self-sufficient. Even after the separation has taken place, the mentor continues to encourage the mentee to move forward in his or her career. In sponsorship mentoring, the mentor will often promote the mentee at a distance and be kept informed of the mentee's progress.

However, some mentors are unwilling to allow their mentees to go beyond their influence and control. This is most common in senior executives who are insecure in their own positions. The mentor tends to project his or her own negative career expectations onto the mentee. If the mentor feels he or she can go no higher in the company, he or she is unlikely to feel that a subordinate will either.

Some managers whose own careers have stagnated and offer little hope for future advancement resent a mentee who has more career opportunities. This kind of mentor does not want the mentee to outstrip him or her and as a result attempts to delay the mentee's movement by insisting the mentee stay in the same position.

Where the mentee feels ready to break the mentoring relationship but is unable to move beyond the mentor's sphere of influence, he or she may feel frustrated, restless and ultimately hostile. This is another argument against the use of the immediate boss as a mentor. While such feelings can be absorbed across departmental boundaries, they may be explosive within the department. Some companies use the personnel department, the mentoring co-ordinator or an arbitrator in senior management to ensure that the mentee has someone to appeal to if conflict of this kind arises. (The mentor, too, can use this formal route to express disquiet if he or she believes a mentee is being pushed too fast for his or her own good.) Such arbitration is rare, however, not least because the numbers of people involved in most companies are sufficiently small for the issues to be resolved by informal means.

For both the mentor and the mentee the period of divorce and separation is important for their reputation and career in the organisation. The mentee demonstrates his or her skills and independence while the mentor shows to colleagues and other potential mentees that he or she develops young people successfully. The progress of the mentee proves the accuracy of the mentor's insight into potential.

By now, the mentee's career objectives may have changed several times as the mentor has made him or her aware of new opportunities and expected changes in the organisation. The mentee will have gradually assumed more and more of the responsibility for his or her own career objectives and will increasingly be taking the initiative in seeking out training opportunities and experience that will help him or her achieve his or her goals. In effect, the mentor has taught what he or she knows and there is little more to pass on.

In developmental mentoring the dynamic is subtly different, not least because it is extremely rare for this kind of dependency to develop in the first place. In a relationship where the primary purpose is achieving rapid self-reliance and where the mentor is not expected to use his or her power on behalf of the mentee, winding down is a relatively straightforward affair. In many cases, where a formal time limit has been built into the scheme from the start, both parties begin to prepare for dissolution long before it starts. (In a mentoring scheme run by Shell, it was noticeable that in the relationships with the least time to run – because the mentor would be repatriated in 12–18 months – the intensity of the relationship and the learning was higher than in those where the time frame was more relaxed. The mentees knew they had to get every drop of learning they could, while they could.)

At least one meeting before the expected formal end of the relationship, mentor and mentee should begin to review:

□ what the relationship has delivered in terms of expected and unexpected outcomes (changes in knowledge, behaviour, role etc) for both parties

□ what it has *not* delivered

□ what they expect for the new (informal) phase of the relationship, if there is to be one

    ◻  what future mentoring needs the mentee may have that may best be met by other people.

## Restarting the relationship

In Kram's analysis both mentee and mentor continue to have some form of interaction, although it is on a more casual basis. The relationship enters a new stage where the mentee and mentor regard each other as equals. The relationship now develops into a friendship with the two maintaining contact with each other on the basis of mutual advantage rather than upon the primarily one-sided career advantage once offered.

The mentee now ceases to identify with the mentor, whose weaknesses he or she now recognises alongside the strengths that had seemed so impressive in the early stages of the relationship. The bond of gratitude takes over from the bond of need. When the two become peers in the organisation, uncertainty and discomfort may occur as they adjust to the new role relationship.

This new transition can also be characterised by hostility and resentment between the mentee and the mentor. The mentee may have found it difficult to make a complete break from the mentor. When the two meet again on a more equal footing, the mentee often feels that he or she will fall into the former dependent role. To prevent this, the mentee behaves aggressively to the mentor and the former intimacy is not re-established.

In developmental mentoring, a similar but gentler transition occurs. Mentor and mentee often continue to meet, but now informally, with no organisational support, no agenda, and much lower frequency. When they do meet, it is as equals, whatever their relative status in the organisation – each sees the other as a useful sounding-board and a valuable person in their networks.

In developmental mentoring, the relationship tends to evolve naturally into a broad friendship, where mentor and mentee recognise each other as one of their learning resources and as mutual sounding-boards. Meetings will be much more spontaneous and relaxed, less frequent, less focused, often based upon the fact that they both happen to be in the same place at the same time.

## Summary

Clearly, every mentoring relationship is unique, just as every individual is unique. But a high proportion of relationships do seem to follow either the Kram stages of development if it is a sponsoring mentoring scheme, or the European four-phase model if it is a developmental scheme. In either case, to minimise the problems and maximise the benefits of mentoring, both the mentor and the mentee need to be well briefed on how the relationship may develop. The company, too, needs to monitor the stages of development to provide the external support that will head off serious problems before they occur.

# 10 PROBLEMS OF MENTORING PROGRAMMES AND RELATIONSHIPS

While mentoring is a powerful human resource development tool, it is only one of many in the corporate toolbox. Badly handled, it can turn into a spanner in the works. Even well handled, it is not appropriate in all circumstances, nor is it necessarily superior to other forms of management development. Rather, it is a process to be used alongside other, more traditional forms of career progression. Many companies that have been running mentoring programmes during the past decade now encourage managers to have as many developmental relationships of different kinds as possible.

Katherine Kram (1983) puts the negative side of a whole-hearted corporate commitment to mentoring:

> The concept has become too aggrandized. Mentoring can sometimes be limited in value or even destructive in a company. Career development staff should remember that other relationships, for example with peers, can be just as rewarding and fruitful as mentoring relationships.

(Note the assumption that peers don't mentor each other!)

Some companies have found the main problem is the unfamiliarity of mentoring in the business environment. Other critics say true mentor-mentee relationships are rare and should not develop at gun-point. Michael Zey, in his book *The Mentor Connection*, feels that trying to formalise 'what is at best a random occurrence' can prove disastrous if management does not stand by the newly joined couples.

Some formal mentoring is seen as a quick fix for companies who should really be looking at changing their whole culture. Reba Keele, Assistant Professor of Organizational Behavior at Brigham Young University, Utah, feels that formal mentoring, like arranged marriages, works better in Far Eastern cultures than Western. In Japan especially, she points out, the traditional respect for age and experience provides a framework that most people can accept:

> In the Japanese organization, the senior member of management has already accepted the fact that he is not going to become the next president. Assuming the responsibility of mentoring is considered an honor and recognition of your status. Whereas in our organizations, issues that have to do with human resource development are not considered primary functions.

Organisations should monitor the programme carefully so that they can identify and solve problems swiftly. Most difficulties can easily be resolved if they are recognised early and brought out into the open. Clear lines of communication between mentors, mentees and programme co-ordinators can ensure that dissatisfactions with the relationship will result in immediate action.

We can divide the most common pitfalls into those that concern the programme and those that concern the individual mentoring relationship.

## Organisational issues

### *Poor planning and preparation*

Unclear programme objectives, failure to gain the public endorsement of senior managers, and under-resourcing the programme are all common failings. A division of a large US-based multinational insisted that its operations around the world all instituted mentoring programmes for a particular group of employees before the year end, a mere four months away. The number of relationships established would be measured and 'heads would roll' if the policy were not implemented enthusiastically. Of course, local senior management responded on the hoof, informing several hundred people in the UK alone that they would be mentor or mentee to someone else. As no one knew what they were doing and there had been no time to gain participants' buy-in, most of the relationships got off to a rocky start. As long as it measured only the number of assigned pairings, the US head office was happy. Only when it started to look at the frequency and quality of meetings did it realise that all but a small handful of the relationships were anything more than a sham.

### Poor clarity of role

Failure to distinguish between the roles of the line manager and the mentor leads to confusion and sometimes to conflict between mentor and line manager. Expecting the mentor to take part in appraising the mentee can also be confusing, on both sides, and lead the mentee to be very cautious about what he or she says. However, it is possible to be quite ingenious in managing this kind of potential conflict of role. At Perot Systems, where most employees work in multiple teams, there is often no single stable point of supervision to carry out an appraisal. Instead, the individual's mentor – or in some cases, the individual – gathers appraisal feedback from a mixture of the mentee's peers, project team leaders and internal customers. This information becomes neutral information – not the mentor's opinion – which the mentor helps the mentee deal with. In this way, there is no need for the mentee to 'play up' to the mentor.

### Failure to set and measure clear outcomes

Many schemes get introduced because someone thinks it would be generally a good thing. So it might, but in the absence of clear expected outcomes, the scheme may easily fall into disrepute as just another talking-shop.

While mentoring may not involve a lot of direct cost, it does require a lot of valuable management time. Top management is justified in asking for some kind of demonstrated return on the investment. Schemes that build in relevant measurement from the start have arguably a better chance of securing and retaining top management support.

### Too little or too much formality

A mentoring scheme aimed at helping children from deprived backgrounds develop literacy and numeracy skills initially required every mentor and mentee to complete a six-page detailed report after each meeting. It hadn't occurred to the organisers that the target audience of mentees might be intimidated by all this. Getting the balance right between formality and informality isn't easy. There has to be enough formality to create a supportive framework, in which relationships can flourish, but enough informality for each mentoring pair to develop its own relationship as it feels fit. Paradoxically, the better trained the mentors and mentees are, the more confident both they and the organisation can feel in allowing relationships to develop in their own way.

### Failure to quality-control the mentor pool

It is now generally regarded as good practice to insist that mentoring relationships will only be sanctioned and supported by the organisation if the mentor and mentee have both attended at least a minimal level of training. Some companies use the mentor training sessions as subtle assessment centres for the mentors – people who demonstrate a complete unsuitability for the role can have their cards marked and, unless somebody specifically asks for them as a mentor, will never be drawn from the pool. These companies also take the view that anyone who volunteers as a mentor should be allowed to attend the training. First, some of the skills and techniques may rub off on them and be used in their dealings with their direct reports; second, they may decide to become a mentee rather than a mentor. On several occasions when the latter has occurred, the person concerned has grown in the role of mentee, using his or her own mentor as a role model for his or her own attempts at acquiring better developmental skills and eventually become an effective mentor.

Where any old manager, selected by seniority rather than developmental competence, is placed into the role, it requires a strong mentee to demand and obtain the kind of deep dialogue he or she needs. The relationship may also require a considerable input of time by the programme co-ordinator, which might be better spent elsewhere. A curious logic often operates in large corporations, however: 'We are a world-class company, employing highly intelligent, world-class people. So all of our senior managers should by definition be good at developing other people. So they should all become mentors.' If all promotions were truly made because managers were good at the people skills, this logic might – just – stand up. But the reality is that managers still primarily get promoted for task achievement and organisational ability, rather than for their skills at developing others. Once a very senior person takes on the title of mentor, there may be little appetite from the mentee, the scheme co-ordinator or anyone else to tell them that they are not doing a good job. The mentor bumbles along in blissful ignorance, the mentee feels trapped and, if there are enough people in the same situation, a deep cynicism about the whole approach establishes itself. These managers may also help to perpetuate stereotypes both in a company's management style and in its culture. Ideas and values that senior executives pass down to mentees may in reality be obsolete or irrelevant. If these values are too vigorously imposed, junior employees are discouraged from finding their own methods and instead use old solutions for new problems. As a result, the company becomes entrenched in the past and loses its ability to react quickly to the demands of the present.

## Being too elitist

Some programmes for high-flyers deliberately set out to be elitist. They want participants to recognise that being chosen as a mentee is a mark of the company's confidence in their potential. There is a downside, however – what about those left out? Since most organisations have a pyramidal structure, it follows that there will always be some junior managers who have a mentor and some who do not. There are just not enough mentors to go round, so a company faces the constant danger of alienating failed candidates.

Unfortunately, the resentment and disappointment felt by failed applicants can outweigh the benefits that successful candidates receive from the programme. A junior who does not gain entry all too often believes the selectors' decision to be based on his or her own personal limitations, rather than due to a lack of programme resources. He or she believes that it is an unspoken statement by the company indicating that he or she lacks the ability to fill important positions in the future. In short, he or she has been given a vote of 'no confidence'.

One UK company with a number of geographically spread operations invited applications for the pilot of its mentoring programme. More than 40 people applied for the 15 available places. Although the company wrote to all the unsuccessful candidates, suggesting they speak to their local employee counsellor, only one did so – and she handed in her notice. The company learned that it had to:

☐ make sure everyone knew the criteria for selection
☐ demonstrate that mentoring was just one route to advancement among many

☐ consider unsuccessful candidates' reactions at a much earlier
stage.

Such negative experiences can be very damaging to a junior
manager. His or her self-confidence and morale may be eroded
to such an extent as to underrate his or her own ability and
potential, and to lower his or her career aspirations accordingly.
As a result, instead of having a motivated young employee who
aims at promotion through a high standard of work, a company
has an individual whose enthusiasm is curbed and who ceases
to stretch his or her abilities because there seems to be no
reward in doing so.

Alternatively, a failed candidate can feel resentment and bitterness as he or she sees peers receive treatment that seems
'preferential'. 'Favouritism' is a frequently heard complaint, as
well as the accusation that peers used unfair tactics to gain a
place on the programme. A mentee's friendship with a senior
executive becomes 'sucking up' or 'crawling'. Envy and resentment from a mentee's peers can frequently hinder, or even
destroy, a mentoring programme.

It is probably not possible to assure everyone that the selection process for high-flyer mentoring has been totally fair, and
there will always be a few individuals who convince themselves
that the programme caters only for those who are best at
impressing the right people rather than those who are most able
and deserving.

## *Being too problem-focused*

When young graduates on the Bank of England's mentoring programme failed to meet their mentors as frequently as expected
and failed to gather much value from the relationship, investigation showed that there were two main causes. One was a
reluctance to disturb someone more senior and obviously very
busy, with their own relatively trivial issues. The other was a
perception that mentors were there to help you deal with problems, rather than to help you identify and manage opportunities. These highly intellectually capable young men and women
perceived that it was not career-enhancing behaviour to admit
weaknesses to anyone else in the organisation, even within a
relationship of confidentiality. Greater clarity at the beginning

about how mentors could add value to their personal development and career planning might have overcome some of these problems, along perhaps with a deferment of the programme until they had been with the bank long enough to develop their own ideas about how they would use a mentor and what sort of mentor would best suit them.

## Power alignments

Primarily a problem of sponsorship mentoring, the issue of power underlies a whole raft of common problems with mentoring schemes. For example, by assigning a mentor to a mentee in a different department or a different division, a company changes the nature of its informal structure. Close relationships that extend beyond the normal business restraints and that cut across the barrier of status and position mean that new alliances are formed between junior and senior employees. A company that has run a mentoring programme for several years may have the additional power nexus of a former mentor and a mentee, now on the same organisational rung, actively promoting and assisting each other. While this means the informal communications of a company are strengthened, it can also lead to an increase in corporate politics.

One of the objectives of the mentoring programme is at least partly to overcome the unfairness of the informal old boy networks. Unless the company is vigilant, there is a very real danger that instead of making the system more open and fair, the scheme may simply create new closed networks. If covert sources of information are available only to the chosen few within mentor-mentee relationships, only the initiated know how to gain and use company resources effectively. Through this, mentors and mentees can form a small yet powerful group capable of operating through and beyond the company's formal positions of power.

Before BP Chemicals began its mentoring programme, doubters thought it would interfere with the authority and skills of the line manager and would set up a network independent of management control. In practice, these fears proved groundless, to the extent that the pilot plant's managers changed from sceptics to enthusiasts.

Failure to make it clear from the outset that the young

person is still primarily responsible to his or her immediate boss and not to his or her mentor can create serious power-play problems. The mentor has to guard against creating situations where the mentee uses his or her special relationship to bypass the authority of his or her boss. At the same time, the mentor must not override the mentee's boss, other than in exceptional cases. Unfortunately, obscuring the company's command structure can happen all too easily. Because the mentor and mentee are adhering to a different system of loyalty and authority, they cut across the recognised formal hierarchy. An invisible chain of command can emerge subtly to challenge the established one, resulting in confusion, conflict and bitterness.

The mentee's immediate superior can often be placed in an uncomfortable and difficult position by all this. A brittle relationship can develop between the mentee, the manager and the mentor if the manager is completely excluded from the relationship, perhaps only learning about it by accident. The manager in this situation feels threatened and frequently resents the mentor's behaviour, interpreting it as open interference. If the mentor overrides the manager's authority, the latter will feel his or her authority is being publicly undermined. Inevitably, the manager will resort to obstructing the mentoring relationship in order to protect his or her own position. An experienced mentoring scheme administrator, quoted in a US newsletter, points out that it's only natural for the mentee's boss, who after all has a department to run, to be jealous of the mentor's influence – especially if the mentor has a powerful position in the organisation. 'Remember that the boss is the boss,' he advises would-be mentors. 'And don't let your own experiences blind you to the realities. The last thing a mentee needs is advice from the mentor that leads to conflict with the supervisor.'

Had the line manager been involved in the programme from the beginning, he might have been more co-operative. It is important that the mentor and line manager should not be seen to collude together, or even to discuss the mentee (this would make it difficult for the mentee to give full trust to the mentor). One company asks line managers to take prospective mentees to the mentor's office for the first meeting. In another, line managers and mentors are briefed together.

In companies where there are a large number of middle

manager positions and few senior positions, mentors again need to conduct their mentoring relationships carefully. A manager who is unlikely to be promoted further may resent the mentee beneath him or her being groomed for advancement. The manager will realise he or she has been passed over by the company and could possibly attempt to hinder the mentee's prospects by writing unfavourable reports. In this situation the mentor and the mentee need to try to make the relationship between them as invisible as possible.

## Relationship issues

### *Failure to establish rapport*

In general, if two people don't 'click' within the first two meetings, the relationship is unlikely to develop the depth of trust and mutual confidence that allows mentor and mentee to address intimate issues. Having a clear developmental goal to work on (ie the mentee's learning, support or career needs) provides a significant boost to the rapport-building process – if only because it provides a clear, shared point of reference and interest. You can learn to value, like and respect someone relatively easily if you work with him or her on something that is important to you.

The reality is, however, that some relationships are not going to work. For example, a middle-aged engineer found he simply could not develop rapport with a highly assertive young woman graduate. Part of the problem, he admitted, was that he kept slipping back into behavioural routines he had developed with his daughter, who was of a similar age and temperament. These routines typically involved a lot of telling and a fair amount of shouting. This was potentially an ideal opportunity for some reverse mentoring, in which he would have learned from the graduate how to understand his daughter's perspective, but he decided to withdraw from the programme altogether.

Rapport demands that both parties share or at least acknowledge the validity of each other's values. In the absence of this consensus, it is always better to dissolve the relationship and help the mentee find someone with whom he or she is more compatible.

### Lack of time

All mentoring relationships suffer from time and diary pressures – in every survey of mentoring problems I have seen, time is one of the top three issues. By definition, people who have the most wisdom to pass on are likely to be among the busiest. Mentees may also be drawn from amongst ambitious groups of people who are themselves working long hours. Yet both mentors and mentees typically do find the time.

In general, it seems, the people who don't make the time are those who don't have the commitment and who don't get the buzz out of reflective dialogue and increasing self-knowledge. Other people find ways around the problem, for example by developing a rolling three-meeting schedule so that a change of date one month does not lead to diary drift the next.

Sometimes what looks like a dead relationship is simply suffering from an overwhelming demand on the mentor's time. In a multinational telecom company, one of a batch of international cross-border relationships hadn't got anywhere after four months. The mentee had chased the mentor frequently, but had only received short e-mails in reply. Then, on the day of a review session, the mentee reported enthusiastically that he had at last spent some telephone time with his mentor, who apologised profusely and explained he had been moved suddenly to take up a major post in another country. Now that he was settled in, however, he was determined to make the relationship work and would fly to Europe in a week or so specifically to hold the first formal meeting.

### Clarity of relationship purpose

If mentor and mentee don't agree fairly quickly on some goals that the mentee would like to achieve and on which the mentor can help, the relationship will swiftly drive into the sand. It doesn't matter that the goals change over time – the sense of purpose drives the frequency of meetings and the focus on real issues.

### Expecting too much of each other

If either the mentor or mentee brings a set of unrealistic expectations to the relationship, this is unlikely to be helpful. In theory, the initial discussions and psychological contract should clarify expectations at all levels. But poor mentors often fail to carry the process through. For example, according to Katherine Kram (1983), when the mentee realises the mentor is unable to transform his or her career, the mentee may feel resentful and betrayed.

Mentees need to be realistic from the beginning, she says. They should not expect the relationship to meet every need, nor for it to continue indefinitely. 'Mentors provide different degrees of mentoring and the mentee should accept this,' she maintains.

Some mentors cross a fine line too easily between exhibiting confidence in a mentee and expecting too much. One young executive was forced to leave his job because of the unbearable pressure his mentor unknowingly placed upon him. He explains:

> He seemed to think I could do anything that he asked me to do. Eventually it got to the stage where I was terrified he would discover I was not a whiz kid and was in fact quite average. My position was made so unbearable by my mentor that I decided to quit.

Had his mentor directed him towards additional training in key areas he might well have gained the confidence to cope.

### Allowing dependency to develop

Primarily an issue for sponsorship mentoring, dependency is unhealthy for both parties. Kram (1983) provides the example of a divisional manager who wished to move to headquarters and could not understand why the company was so reluctant to transfer him:

> I begged the powers that be to move me, yet they refused to alter their position. I was mystified until a colleague told me that my mentor had insisted that I was not ready for the move. The only thing I could do was to make it clear to him that I was grateful for all the help he had given my career, yet nevertheless I was determined to move on – or move out. He denied any involvement, but a month later I was transferred. The evidence seemed to speak for itself.

### Problems with other people

The literature on mentoring contains a variety of references to problems with spouses, line managers and working colleagues. Most of these can be avoided by being very open about the relationship.

Problems with spouses tend to be most common with mixed-gender mentoring relationships, for obvious reasons. These relationships can also generate malicious gossip. Experienced mentors avoid these problems by having a number of mentees of both sexes and by holding meetings relatively publicly.

Problems with line managers occur most often when the line manager feels threatened. Is the mentee bad-mouthing him or her to someone more senior? Is the mentor – perhaps from the best of motives – using his or her position of greater seniority to give the mentee developmental tasks that prevent the mentee spending essential time on line responsibilities? The potential for conflict is substantial, yet most organisations avoid it. Some, such as BP Chemicals, involve the line manager to the extent of taking the mentee to meet the mentor for the first time. Others ensure that mentors and line managers are fully briefed about their respective roles.

A lot of problems with other employees can be overcome by providing clear briefings about the nature of mentoring and how it fits into the portfolio of development opportunities. A pilot programme should always be marketed as such, with a clear statement that if it is successful, it will be rolled out to as many other groups as possible. (That gives everyone who is envious a reason to help make the scheme work!)

## Summary

Mentoring should not be the only form of career or personal development within the organisation. The company must also be aware of the problems and the conflicts that the mentoring pair may experience with the mentee's boss and peers. Careful selection and preparation of both mentor and mentee can avoid both these problems and others that may arise with the mentoring relationship itself.

# 11 DIVERSITY MENTORING

When I first wrote *Everyone Needs a Mentor*, the concept of using mentoring as a vehicle for promoting equal opportunity was still fairly new. The handful of programmes there were tended to focus on high-potential women. Since then, several evolutions have occurred. One is that mentoring for equal opportunity at work now addresses a wide range of target groups, from women at all levels and career stages, through ethnic minorities, to the mentally and physically disabled. The other is that the concept of equal opportunity has to a significant extent been overtaken by diversity management. Where equal opportunity attempts to redress the power balance in the workplace in favour of previously disadvantaged groups, diversity management takes the more positivist view that organisations should be making the maximum use of the diversity of cultures, skills, genders and personalities within them.

These two views, which are not necessarily incompatible, tend to inform how companies design their mentoring programmes. For many, the most practical approach is a programme aimed specifically at a clearly defined group. Aer Rianta, the Irish Airports Authority, achieved significant results over a number of years with a programme to link women in junior and middle management with male executives (there not being any female executives at the time). An Post, the Irish Post Office, recently embarked on a similar scheme, but using mentors drawn from key customers and suppliers. The problems with such an approach, however, include the following:

☐ There is the possibility that many potential participants don't want to be labelled in this way, as BP Engineering found when it consulted a cross-section of its female employees. Rather, they wanted to be encouraged to join a wider scheme, open to all, which would not carry the stigma of disadvantage.

☐ There is the difficulty of defining just who is disadvantaged (is a black female with an Oxbridge education more disadvantaged than a white male with a poor education and from a lower-class background?) and who belongs to a group. One North American company was embarrassed when homosexual employees complained that the women's leadership programme disadvantaged them, so the company formed another scheme, only to find that other groups, such as the physically disabled, also wanted the same privileges. Confused by a plethora of schemes, potential mentors backed away in droves. The company attempted to place all the disadvantaged groups into one scheme, but some groups didn't want to be categorised alongside others they considered different. The process collapsed under the weight of bureaucracy and now anyone, from any group, including the most positively advantaged, can apply for a mentor.

☐ How valid are the assumptions about behavioural change? For example, a gender-based glass ceiling programme defined its mentoring element in terms of helping women understand how to think and behave at a more senior level. Some of the women challenged this definition and asked for an analysis of what behaviours they needed to acquire. It soon became clear that cloning male executives might not meet the programme goal, as a high proportion of the male executives did not exemplify these behaviours either. Indeed, in many cases the female mentees were better exemplars of those behaviours than their intended mentors. Redefining the programme to legitimise building on the strengths the women had, rather than change them into something else, gave a stronger sense of commitment and purpose.

Mentoring aimed to support diversity management overcomes most of these problems, but it makes it much more difficult to target mentoring on people who will particularly benefit from it. Companies taking this approach tend to develop practical methods to encourage people to come forward – for example, by making mentoring an option to be considered at each performance appraisal.

## Same group, different group?

One of the most controversial issues in diversity mentoring is whether the mentor should be from the same group or a different group.

A strong practical reason against same-group mentoring in many organisations is that there aren't enough people from the minority or disadvantaged group to meet the demand. Given that two or at most three mentees per mentor is the maximum recommended, there will frequently be a supply and demand problem. One of the major mistakes organisations make is to press into service the handful of senior managers who are black or female (or both), regardless of whether they have the aptitude and interest to be an active and effective mentor.

There seem to be five key aspects to the arguments around this issue. The first is *perspective* – whether and how the mentor can help the mentee view his or her issues in a manner useful to learning. The mentor from a different group – especially if he or she is also at a higher level in the organisation – can provide a very different set of viewpoints. If the mentor comes from the powerful majority, he or she may be better at explaining how the system functions and how to work with it, rather than against it. The mentor is able to help the mentee see barriers and opportunities in ways that make them easier to tackle. For example, a young Muslim mentee was having great difficulty adapting to working in a multinational organisation. He expected to be given frequent, clear instructions and to report back to his supervisor constantly. Instead, he found that the supervisor responded with: 'Look, you know what to do. Why don't you just get on with it?' As a result, relationships between them were very strained, especially when the mentee was passed over for a promotion.

Working with the mentor, this young man gradually came to understand what the supervisor's expectations were and the value the organisation placed upon self-reliance and demonstrating initiative. He also worked out how to fit in with the organisation's behavioural expectations, while not sacrificing any of the values important to him from his own culture. He rehearsed with the mentor how he would discuss these issues with his supervisor to build a better understanding between them.

While a difference of perspective was important here, in other cases the dominant need may be for greater empathy. The white mentor above could not easily put himself in the mentee's shoes – he had never been in such a situation. Same-group mentors can extend greater understanding. One of the classic examples is the experiment by part of the Prudential in the UK to assist returning mothers with a mentor. The mentor – a mum who had made the same transition within recent years – contacted the employee some months ahead of the return date and worked with her for several months until she had settled back in again. The mentor in this case was able to share the feelings of guilt, inadequacy and being pulled in too many directions, which so many returning mothers feel. 'Being able to talk with someone who had been there and come through it made all the difference,' said one mentee.

The second key aspect is *networking*. The mentor from the dominant group is likely to be much better connected, and even a mentor who is not in the power structure will be able to introduce the mentee to very different people. The same-group mentor is likely to have networks that largely overlap with those of the mentee.

*Power* is the third aspect. Minority group mentors are less likely to be in senior positions, so they cannot provide either the depth of understanding of the organisation (another result of perspective) or – in sponsorship mentoring – the potential to exert influence on the mentee's behalf. If the mentee is ambitious, there is much to be learned from someone who has developed the skills of acquiring and using power wisely.

Being a *role model* is also an important consideration. Same-group mentors may be more likely to reinforce attitudes and behaviours that are not valued by the organisation. Different-group mentors can provide role models for behaviours that are valued. (However, it may not always be possible for the mentee to distinguish between appropriate and inappropriate role models – having a mentor from *both* groups may provide greater insight.)

In deciding whether the relationship should be constructed within the same group or across different groups, then, a variety of issues need to be taken into account. The most fundamental, however, is *what is the mentee's need*? If support is the most critical need, then a same-group mentor may be most appropriate. If being stretched is the goal, then a mentor from a different group is likely to be most effective. In addition, it should be remembered that the mentor is not the only potential source of learning for the mentee – the wider the learning net the mentee can create, the more he or she can receive of both nurture and challenge.

## Positioning diversity

The increasing numbers of women and minorities now entering careers in management suffer from a major disadvantage: by and large they are not exposed to the same range of experiences and career opportunities as men. While formal barriers have been reduced through legislation, they continue to be hindered in their careers by invisible obstacles such as prejudice and distrust. As the demand for quality white-collar management increases, the need for organisations to question why there are so few women and minorities in management will become acute.

If these managers are accepted in the formal structure of the organisation, in the informal social structure they can still be looked on with suspicion. For example, the masculine culture of a company may mean that women are not fully integrated; in a sense they are still regarded as outsiders or interlopers.

Low expectations or stereotyped images can often mean that women and minority managers are delegated undemanding jobs, making them less visible than white male managers. Women may be expected to perform tasks that are seen as suitably 'feminine' in nature, such as personnel, rather than the more 'masculine' managerial jobs, such as financial analysis. As a result, women managers frequently lack opportunities to develop a wide range of managerial skills.

In the UK, I carried out some years ago a survey of business women, with questionnaires sent to 100 who had reached executive level inside a company and to 100 women entrepreneurs. The response rate was a remarkable 49 per cent. Among the key conclusions were the following:

☐ Successful women managers are more likely than women entrepreneurs to have had a mentor (56 per cent compared

with 43 per cent). One reason – possibly the most important
– is that the entrepreneurs quit to set up on their own pre-
cisely because their progress was blunted in large corporations, through lack of a champion at higher levels.

□ Forty-nine per cent of the women had had a single mentor;
22 per cent had had two; 21 per cent had had three; and 8 per
cent had had four or five – or more – at different periods in
their careers.

□ Ninety-four per cent of the women said their relationships
were beneficial to their career.

□ More than half of the entrepreneurs' mentors had encouraged
them to start their own businesses; 5 per cent even helped
them financially.

□ The vast majority of mentoring relationships (63 per cent)
started accidentally; only 8 per cent of the women had actually approached their mentor.

□ The main benefits reported by the women were:
  – improved self-confidence and self-image
  – increased visibility to senior management (especially
    important to women managers)
  – focusing career aspirations
  – acting as a role model
  – help with work problems
  – improved communications and skills.

□ Most mentors (79 per cent) were male.

□ More than two-fifths experienced no problems with the relationship; 37 per cent had experienced problems of resentment from peers; 5 per cent said their careers had been
damaged when their mentor lost credibility in the company.

□ Two-thirds had experienced some form of sexual innuendo or
gossip; 19 per cent reported that their mentor's wife felt
threatened by the relationship; 11 per cent said their own
husbands resented it; 4 per cent said their mentor became too
emotionally involved with them.

□ Sixty per cent of the women were acting as mentors themselves.

Dr Judi Marshall of Bath University found that mentoring
improved the promotion prospects of women managers.

Interviewing 30 women managers from middle management to director level, Marshall found that 70 per cent either were currently or had been in a mentoring relationship. All of these women placed great value on the relationship and said it had been a very important factor in their career development, she explained. The majority of the surveyed women saw visibility as a crucial factor for success. The mentors sponsored the women and often nominated them for promotion committees when they would not have normally been considered for posts. If a mentor vouches for a woman manager, companies are more willing to promote her because they view the mentor as a 'safety net', she concludes.

Jenny Blake, an independent consultant, comments:

> I think the mentoring relationship is very beneficial to both the mentee and the mentor. In my capacity as a consultant I now try to fill the mentor role. I mentor personnel trainers and help them with their own development. At the moment I am mentoring a senior manager in the probationary service. I feel an older woman can play a very positive role as a mentor. I do not appear threatening to men, so I receive open feedback. I have found that an increasing number of women in their late 30s and 40s are now willing to be mentors. They want to act as a role model to younger women to demonstrate that women can succeed in business. It seems clear to me that mentoring can and will play a very positive role in the future.

## Potential problems with male/female mentoring

### Between the mentee and the mentor

A female mentee often experiences disappointment with the relationship because her male mentor is unable to meet all her developmental needs. She cannot emulate him fully and in certain areas may need to find her own methods of achieving goals and resolving problems. Women put more emphasis than men on delegating or on group discussion. If the male mentor does not understand this, he may interpret it as lack of assertiveness and push the female mentee into signing up for an assertiveness course.

Sexual tensions between the two can inhibit the relationship and make it less rewarding than mentoring between two of the same sex.

Pressure to adopt established sexual roles sometimes causes tension and conflict in the relationship. A male mentor may feel overly protective towards a female mentor and encourage her to be dependent. She may find it particularly difficult to terminate the relationship at the end of the mentoring programme. The same may also be true in the case of a female mentor and male mentee, especially where the age differences are similar to those in a mother/son relationship.

Says Dr Marilyn Puder-York, a clinical psychologist in New York:

> There are many very productive male-female mentoring relationships, but there must be a high sense of shared values and ethical behaviour on both sides.
>
> And you often have to counter society's perception of the relationship by having lunch instead of dinner and by including spouses in socialising. Otherwise both can pay a heavy price. In general, if a woman has a male mentor, she should seek out a woman mentor as well. Beyond the social considerations, there are politics for women that a man may not be aware of.

### Between the spouses and the mentoring pair

A mentoring relationship can seem threatening to the mentor's and mentee's partners, especially if business trips together are involved. The spouse often feels excluded by the closeness of the relationship.

Mentees have found various solutions, mostly based on total openness. Social gatherings where spouses are invited make a useful opportunity to demonstrate the businesslike nature of the relationship.

### Between the company and the mentoring pair

Sexual gossip and innuendo can kill a mentoring relationship before it gets going. Many potential male/female mentoring relationships never happen because of the fear of office gossip. In a mentoring programme it is often necessary for the two to work beyond work hours or even travel together. The two must act 'professionally', which can simply mean that behaviour has to be much more circumscribed than in a mentor relationship between two of the same sex. One mentor solved the problem of gossip: 'If you mentor one woman you are branded as a womaniser. If you mentor several, you are praised for your commitment to seeing more women in management.'

The extra visibility of the relationship in the company may discourage even the highest risk-taker from being a mentor: 'A young man can have the luxury of failing quietly but a woman's mistakes are often broadcast,' explains one mentor.

## Mentoring across racial/cultural divides

Mentoring between races requires equally sensitive handling. The potential for stereotyping to reduce the effectiveness of the relationship is high; as too is the potential to identify and over-come stereotypes. In experiments across cultures, I have found it is important to begin the relationship with an extra dose of clarity about expectations. On one occasion, in Brunei, man-agers being trained as mentors were asked to plot the shape of the relationship in terms of where the emphasis of behaviours should rest. Figure 13 shows what the expatriate (English and Dutch) mentors concluded.

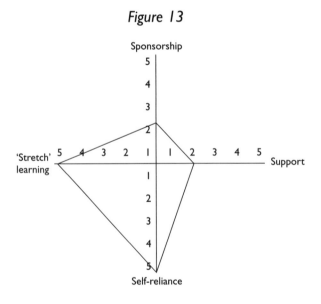

*Figure 13*

Figure 14 shows what the mentees, who were mostly local people in their mid-twenties, were expecting.

*Figure 14*

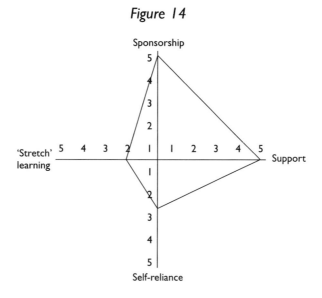

After nearly two minutes of silence one manager exclaimed, 'Now I see why I have such difficulty getting through to my direct reports!' Mentors and mentees used this information to discuss what behaviours and expectations on both sides would be appropriate, and to build a compromise acceptable to both parties.

Like mentoring across genders, mentoring across cultures is an excellent developmental experience for the mentor. Some companies now encourage such relationships as an integral part of globalising their cultures.

## Summary

Mentoring for diversity is one of the most positive developments in organisational learning in recent years. It benefits the disadvantaged employee, for whom doors begin to open up; it benefits the mentor, who learns how to interact with and get the most from employees of widely differing backgrounds; and it benefits the company by making much more effective use of the talent available.

# 12  EXECUTIVE MENTORING[1]

One area where mentoring has grown very rapidly has been at the very top of organisations. Although a few companies, such as engineers T&N, have experimented with peer mentoring between directors, and others, such as Diageo, have developed a cadre of HR professionals whose main role is to coach and/or mentor the top 100 or so people, most mentoring of executives and directors is carried out by external mentors, who are often professionals in the role.

## The growing popularity of mentoring

So why has executive mentoring suddenly become so popular?

Among the stimuli for the executive mentoring movement are (Clutterbuck and Schneider 1998):

☐ *A gradual repositioning of the nature and role of mentoring at this level.* The UK, along with most other Western nations, has a tradition of high-level mentoring with strong sponsorship overtones. As you set your sights on the executive suite, you seek an elder statesperson who can actively steer your progress, find opportunities that will increase your visibility, make introductions and generally be influential on your behalf. Given that most people prefer to be seen as having succeeded by their own efforts, it is hardly surprising that they were sometimes reluctant to acknowledge the mentor's role and contribution.

☐ The rapid spread of *developmental* mentoring in the past 10 years, especially among graduates and minorities, has gradually changed the perception of mentoring in general – at least in the UK and Europe. This is much more in keeping with the image executives are comfortable to project, especially when they are expected to be a role model to others.

- At the same time, there is an *increasing acceptance that development is a continuous, career-long activity*, even (perhaps especially) at the top. Time pressures make it very difficult for executives to attend business school seminars frequently, and much of the training provided both in such courses and within their organisations is at too low a level to be immediately relevant to their needs. Executives learn most intensively from working on real issues, business or personal, in small groups or one to one.

- *Changes in the nature of executive roles.* Senior managers and directors operate in an increasingly complex and stressful environment. Constant organisational change demands constant personal change at the top. For the executive to maintain his or her pace of personal change alongside that of the organisation, he or she needs someone else who can goad, support, ask penetrating questions and be a kind of 'development conscience'. This is particularly true in smaller businesses, where a major cause of failure is that the business grows faster than the capabilities of the owner-entrepreneur to manage it.

- *Changing organisation structures.* With flatter hierarchies, the transition from middle to senior manager, or senior manager to director, has become much more of a shock to the system. The learning curve is very steep and anecdotal evidence suggests that, for example, fewer than one in three people who take on the title of director fully absorbs the difference in role. Having someone help you through these major transitions is becoming almost a necessity.

Professional mentors help executives get at their own issues, build their own insights and self-awareness, develop their own, unique ways of handling how they interact with key colleagues and with the business. The professional mentor uses current issues to explore patterns of thinking and behaviour, often starting with the executive's values. They ask penetrating questions that stimulate thinking, challenge the executive to take control of issues avoided, help the executive put his or her own learning in context, and raise his or her ability to cope with new issues, through greater self-understanding and confidence.

To be effective, professional mentors have to have a broad knowledge and exposure to business direction, to the patterns of senior management thinking and behaviour. They must have a store of relevant business, strategic and behavioural models – and the capacity to generate bespoke models on the spot – which can help executives explore the context of issues under discussion. They need exceptional interpersonal skills of their own, together with a more than passing competence in what can broadly be called counselling skills. Not surprisingly, these are relatively rare creatures.

One reason why professional mentoring is so much more demanding – on the executive as well as the mentor – is that it is so holistic. It seeks and deals with issues wherever they are. It requires the mentor to recognise and adapt roles according to the executive's needs at the time. So the mentor may need to be coach, counsellor, sounding-board, critical friend, networker or any of a number of roles, sometimes within the same two-hour session. This constant reassessing and refocusing is helped by addressing the executive's issues from at least three viewpoints – the values and emotions that drive their behaviour and decision-making, the leader-manager style they adopt, and the needs of the business. Among key questions that emerge frequently are (Clutterbuck and Schneider 1998):

- How do you think about this issue? (Is your thinking rigorous enough? Adventurous enough?)
- What do you feel about the issue?
- How does this make you behave? (And how consistent is your behaviour?)
- How do you make things happen? (And what do you do when they do not happen?)
- How well do you understand what is really going on in your team? Your business?
- How well do you understand what happens within you? (Do you need to develop greater self-awareness? Can you increase your 'emotional intelligence'?)
- How could you contribute more? (Not just in the business, but to your own well-being and that of other people?)

## Summary

Executive mentoring is a rapidly expanding area of practice. Most activity occurs through external provision, not least because senior managers find it hard to open out to peers, who may also be rivals for the top jobs. It's quite difficult for many executives to admit their fears and weaknesses to colleagues. A few companies, such as Diageo, have experimented with internal specialists, usually people with a strong behavioural/psychology background who operate with a high degree of independence. However, it is hard to develop the depth of friendship that typifies the really effective mentoring relationship. For those who venture outside the organisation, there is no shortage of willing providers. However, there is often confusion between executive coaching (building a particular skill set) and executive mentoring (thinking through issues more deeply). Moreover, there are no barriers to entry and no widely subscribed set of professional standards. Caveat emptor!

## Endnote

1 Adapted from an article presented in a Croner newsletter, 12 January 1998.

# 13 CONCLUSION

In this relatively brief account of mentoring and how to implement a mentoring programme, we have inevitably raised a number of issues that warrant further discussion. Below we take up some of these in more detail.

## All good mentoring relationships come to an end

While one person may have several mentors, each mentoring relationship must reach the stage where it is neither needed nor wanted any longer.

For this reason it is essential that each relationship is seen from the start as a temporary alignment. Elements of it may persist, in the form of mutual aid and friendship, for many years after, but there must be clear starting- and finishing-points. Probably the best signpost of the finishing-point is when the mentee has achieved the medium-term objectives established early on in the relationship. A spokesperson for Jewel Companies comments:

> We feel that after a couple of years the role loses its importance and may become a more negative element than a positive one. That is, after a few years in the business it is more important that an individual be achieving on his own rather than with the special help from a senior-management-level mentor.

However it is done, the two parties must be able to back out of the arrangement without recrimination where one or both feel it is no longer beneficial.

## Good mentees often make good mentors

Many of the most successful mentors are people who have experienced mentoring from the other side. Indeed, it is possible for a manager to be simultaneously mentored from above while he or she mentors someone yet more junior.

One of the major difficulties in getting a mentoring programme off the ground is finding an adequate supply of mentors. Once the scheme has been going for many years, however, it automatically generates potential mentors from the ranks of former mentees. Indeed, this is one of the litmus tests for the success of a programme – what proportion of mentees want to go on to become mentors?

## Old-stagers can benefit from mentors, too

Mentoring should not be seen solely for young, relatively new recruits. There are frequently people in the organisation whose development has been held back by circumstances other than ability. They may, for example, have had domestic ties that prevented them from demonstrating career ambition, particularly if they are married women. Or they may be in a cultural backwater in the company, out of the mainstream and in a staff position that has little interaction with key corporate functions.

Equally, mentoring relationships can be effective between peers, or from a junior person to someone more senior.

## Finding a mentor when there is no formal mentoring programme

Many people progress in their companies by seeking their own mentors. By and large, senior managers are apt to be flattered if they are convinced the approach comes from someone who is capable of going a long way. The following ground rules may be useful within the corporate context:

### *Target one or two people as potential mentors*

Talk to other people to discover their reputation within the firm. Is this person going places? Is he or she interested in developing other people? Is he or she known for teamwork? Will he or she have time for a mentoring relationship or has he or she just been given a major project that will keep him or her out of the country for six months a year? Build up as accurate a picture as possible of each mentor candidate to establish who could be of most help to you in your career and/or personal development.

### Make yourself visible

It is not who you know that counts, but who knows you. You have to make potential mentors aware of your existence. Use friends, colleagues and acquaintances to identify useful networks to join. Make a point of attending social functions, 'learning breakfasts' and other developmental events.

### Show you have ambition and want to improve your abilities

Establishing the seriousness of your ambition to advance is essential. If the opportunity presents itself, get the senior manager involved in recommending training or reading that will help you expand your experience and knowledge.

### Ask the potential manager formally, in person, to be your mentor

Most managers will be flattered and respond positively to an approach in person, either agreeing or making helpful suggestions as to who else in the company would be more suitable. In the latter case they will often make introductions or recommendations on your behalf. Even if you simply receive a blunt refusal, you have at least established your credentials as an ambitious employee, willing to learn.

More generally, especially if you seek a mentor from the wider community, the following checklist may provide some useful starting-points:

1  *What do you need a mentor for?* Try to clarify what kind of transition you want to make. Is it to a different job? A different level of competence? A different situation in life?

2  *What kind of help do you want?* Do you want someone to be a sounding-board for you, to give encouragement, to provide you with a constructive challenge and expand your horizons, or to 'look out' for you, identifying opportunities and putting you forward for them? You are less likely to find someone if you are looking for a sponsor or someone to do things for you. People are much more likely to respond to a request for sharing their experience.

3  *What sort of person would best be able to help you by giving advice and guidance?* Think about personality, age, experience. Think also about geography – how difficult would it be for the two of you to meet?

4 *What could you bring to the relationship?* Is there any area of knowledge or experience you might usefully offer to share with them?

5 *Who do you know already?* Is there someone in your workplace, your local community, the church, local clubs who you admire and feel you could learn from?

6 *What networks do you belong to?* Are you a member of a professional association, an alumni club, a chamber of commerce, a sports association or similar organisation? They may already have a mentoring scheme, or be willing to put you in touch with potential mentors on an ad hoc basis.

7 *Are there mentor registers you can sign on to?* A variety of organisations, including some TECs, charities and community organisations, provide a matching service for specific categories of people.

8 *Can you identify someone you could approach who is very well networked and could refer you either directly to potential mentors or to organisations that can help?* Someone in any of the organisations above may be able to help you in this way. Other useful people to consider approaching include personnel professionals, senior managers, academic tutors, pastors and career consultants.

9 *How will you make the approach?* It is often easier when someone else will make the introduction. If you have to take the first steps yourself, however, spend some time rehearsing what you have to say. Be confident – the worst that can happen is that they say no. In practice, most people are sufficiently flattered and respond very positively to requests that they should become a mentor.

10 *How will you translate good intentions into deeds?* Aim to put the date for the first formal mentoring meeting into the diary as soon as he or she agrees to consider the relationship. Don't be the one to postpone the meeting – that may undo all your good work. Above all, be considerate of the mentor's time and goodwill – make it clear how pleased you are that he or she has accepted.

# USEFUL CONTACTS

European Mentoring Centre
Burnham House
High Street
Burnham
Bucks SL1 7JZ
Tel: 01628 661919
Website: www.mentoringcentre.org

International Mentoring Association
Western Michigan University
1903 W. Michigan Avenue
Kalamazoo, MI 49008-5201
USA
Tel: +1 616 387 4174
Website: www.wmich.edu/conferences/mentoring/ima.html

National Mentoring Consortium
Mentoring Unit
University of East London
Duncan House
High Street
London E15 2JB
Tel: 020 8223 3000
Website: nmc-online.com

National Mentoring Network
1st Floor, Charles House
Albert Street
Eccles
Manchester M30 0PD
Tel: 0161 787 8600
Website: www.nmn.org.uk

Oxford School of Coaching and Mentoring
Wolsey Hall
66 Banbury Road
Oxford OX2 6PR
Tel: 01865 481442
Website: www.oscm.co.uk

# BIBLIOGRAPHY

ACES NEWSLETTER (1981) 'Mentoring and networking'. December.

ALLEMAN E. (1984a) *Measuring Mentoring: A manual for the leadership development questionnaire*. Available from Leadership Development Consultants INC Mentor, Ohio.

ALLEMAN E. (1984b) *What's really true about mentoring?* Leadership Development Consultants INC Mentor, Ohio.

ALLEMAN E. (1994) 'Interpersonal perceptions in mentoring relationships'. Paper presented at the annual meeting of the American Educational Research Association, New Orleans.

ALLEMAN E., COCHRAN J., DOVERSPIKE J. *and* NEWMAN I. (1984) 'Enriching mentoring relationships'. *The Personnel and Guidance Journal*. February.

BARHAM K. *and* CONWAY C. (1997) 'Mentoring goes international'. *Ashridge Journal*.

BARHAM K. *and* CONWAY C. (1998) *Developing Business and People Internationally: A mentoring approach*. Berkhampstead, Ashridge Research.

BAXTER A. G. *and* CLARK K. M. (1992) 'Positive and productive mentoring: inside views'. *Mentoring International*. Vol. 6, No. 2–3, spring/summer.

BENNETTS C. (1995) 'The secrets of a good relationship'. *People Management*. 30 June.

BENNETTS C. (1996) 'Turning mentoring into a fine art'. *People Management*. 25 January.

BENNETTS C. (1998) *A Pilot Inquiry into Current Mentoring Projects and Programmes for Unemployed Youth in England, Scotland and Wales*. Hertfordshire TEC.

BLAKE R. R. *and* MOUTON J. S. (1964) *The Managerial Grid*. Houston, Texas, Gulf.

BRITISH INSTITUTE OF MANAGEMENT (1987) *Mentoring*. MINT series. February.

BUREAU OF BUSINESS PRACTICE (1990) 'Being a mentor'. *Management Letter 304*. February.

BURKE R. J. (1984) 'Mentors in organizations'. *Group and Organization Studies*. September.

CARTER S. (1993) 'Developing an organisation mentoring scheme'. *Professional Manager*.

CARTER S. *and* LEWIS G. (1994) *The Four Bases of Mentoring*. Proceedings of the First European Mentoring Conference, European Mentoring Centre/Sheffield Business School.

CARUSO R. (ED.) (1992) *Mentoring and the Business Environment: Asset or liability?* Dartmouth, USA.

CHAO G. T. (1998) 'Invited reaction: challenging research in mentoring'. *Human Resource Development Quarterly*. Vol. 9, No. 4, winter.

CHAO G. T., WALZ P. M. *and* GARDNER P. D. (1992) 'Formal and informal mentorships: a comparison of mentoring functions and contrast with non-mentored counterparts'. *Personnel Psychology*. Vol. 45.

CLAWSON J. G. (1985) 'Is mentoring necessary?' *Training and Development Journal*. April.

CLUTTERBUCK D. (1992) *Top Manager Programme*. Oxford, Regional Health Authority.

CLUTTERBUCK D. (1993) *Mentoring – A key tool in training and development, current best practice*. London, the Industrial Society.

CLUTTERBUCK D. (1994a) 'Blooming managers'. *Management Training*. February.

CLUTTERBUCK D. (1994b) 'Business mentoring in evolution'. *Mentoring*. Summer.

CLUTTERBUCK D. (1994c) 'Managing mentoring, how to avoid the common pitfalls'. *Mentoring and Coaching*. Deventer, Netherlands, Kluwer Bedrijfswetenschappen.

CLUTTERBUCK D. (1994d) 'The mentoring game'. *The Business Magazine*. October.

CLUTTERBUCK D. (1994e) 'Uncovering the way a mentor does his work'. *The Business Magazine*. November.

CLUTTERBUCK D. (1995) *Consenting Adults*. London, Channel Four Publications.

CLUTTERBUCK D. (1996a) 'Developing learning teams'. *Training Officer*. Vol. 32, No. 6, July–August.

CLUTTERBUCK D. (1996b) 'How executives learn from each other'. In P. Sadler (ed.), *International Executive Development Programmes*. London, Kogan Page.

CLUTTERBUCK D. (1996c) 'Will you be my mentor?' *Modern Management*. Vol. 10, June.

CLUTTERBUCK D. (1997a) 'Are you getting in the way of the learning organisation?' *Direction*. April.

CLUTTERBUCK D. (1997b) 'Mentoring and the glass ceiling'. *The*

*Diversity Directory*. 12th edn. Southampton, Diversity UK.

CLUTTERBUCK D. (1997c) *Power in the Mentoring Relationship*. London, Staff and Educational Development Association.

CLUTTERBUCK D. (1998a) *Learning Alliances*. London, Institute of Personnel and Development.

CLUTTERBUCK D. (1998b) 'The rapid rise of executive mentoring'. *Croner's Human Resources Briefing*. 12 January.

CLUTTERBUCK D. (1999a) 'Mentoring, developing two for the price of one'. In J. Prior MBE (ed.), *Gower Handbook of Training and Development*. 3rd edn, Chapter 24, Aldershot, Gower.

CLUTTERBUCK D. (1999b) 'Mentoring in business, executives and directors'. *Mentoring and Tutoring*. Vol. 6, No. 3.

CLUTTERBUCK D. (2000a) 'Ten core mentor competencies'. *Organisations and People*. November, Vol. 7, No. 2.

CLUTTERBUCK D. (2000b) 'Where next in mentoring?' *AMED News*. October.

CLUTTERBUCK D. (2000/2001) 'Quiet transformation, the growing power of mentoring'. *Mount Eliza Business Review*. Summer/autumn.

CLUTTERBUCK D. *and* DEVINE M. (1987) *Businesswoman*. London, Macmillan.

CLUTTERBUCK D. *and* MEGGINSON D. (1999) *Mentoring Executives and Directors*. Oxford, Butterworth-Heinemann.

CLUTTERBUCK D. *and* SCHNEIDER S. (1998) 'Executive mentoring'. *Croner's Executive Companion Bulletin*. October, Issue 29.

CLUTTERBUCK D. *and* SNOW D. (1995) *BEAT – Beginning Education and Training: An evaluation*. Birmingham, BEAT Projects.

CLUTTERBUCK D. *and* WYNNE B. (1993) 'Mentoring and coaching'. In *Handbook of Management Development*. Aldershot, Gower.

COLLIN A. (1979) 'Notes on some typologies of management development and the role of the mentor in the process of adaptation of the individual to the organisation'. *Personnel Review*. Vol. 8, No. 1.

CONWAY C. (1998) *Strategies for Mentoring*. Chichester, John Wiley.

CORPORATE MENTORING SOLUTIONS (CMSI) (2001) *Mentoring Program Benchmark 2001 Survey*. Vancouver, CMSI.

CROSBY F. J. (1999) 'The development literature on developmental relationships', in A. J. Murrell, F. J. Crosby and R. J. Ely (eds), *Mentoring Dilemmas: Developmental relationships within multicultural organizations*. New Jersey, Lawrence Erlbaum Associates.

CUNNINGHAM J. B. *and* EBERLE T. (1993) 'Characteristics of the mentoring experience: a qualitative study'. *Personnel Review*. Vol. 22, No. 4.

DARLING L. A. (1984) 'Mentor types and life cycles'. *The Journal of Nursing Administration*. November.

ENGSTRÖM T. (1997–8) 'Personality factors' impact on success in the mentor-protégé relationship'. MSc thesis to Norwegian School of Hotel Management, Oslo.

FAGAN M. (1988) 'The term "mentor": a review of the literature'. *International Journal of Mentoring*. Vol. 2, No. 12, winter.

FAGENSON-ELAND E. A., MARKS M. A. *and* AMENDOLA (1997) 'Perceptions of mentoring relationships'. *Journal of Vocational Behaviour*. Vol. 51.

FORRET M. L., TURBAN D. B. and DOUGHERTY T. W. (1996) 'Issues facing organisations when implementing formal mentoring programmes'. *Leadership and Organization Journal*. Vol. 17, No. 3.

GARDNER C. (1997) *Mentoring: A professional friendship?* Proceedings of the Fourth European Conference on Mentoring, European Mentoring Centre/Sheffield Business School.

GARVEY R. (1995) 'Healthy signs for mentoring'. *Education and Training*. Vol. 37, No. 5.

GARVEY R. (1998) 'Mentoring in the marketplace: studies of learning at work'. Thesis submitted for the degree of Doctor of Philosophy, Durham University.

GARVEY R. (1999) 'Mentoring and the changing paradigm'. *Mentoring and Tutoring*. Vol. 7, No. 1.

GARVEY R. *and* ALRED G. (2000a) 'Developing mentors'. *Career Development International*.

GARVEY R. *and* ALRED G. (2000b) 'Educating mentors'. *Mentoring and Tutoring*. Vol. 8, No. 2.

GARVEY R., ALRED G. *and* SMITH R. (1996) 'First person mentoring'. *Career Development International*. Vol. 1, No. 5.

GIBB S. (1994a) 'Evaluating mentoring'. *Education and Training*. Vol. 36, No. 5.

GIBB S. (1994b) 'Inside corporate mentoring schemes, the development of a conceptual framework'. *Personnel Review*. Vol. 23, No. 3.

GIBB S. (1999) 'The usefulness of theory, a case study in evaluating formal mentoring schemes'. *Human Relations*. Vol. 52, No. 2, August.

GIBB S. *and* MEGGINSON D. (1992) 'Inside corporate mentoring schemes, a new agenda of concerns'. *Personnel Review*. Vol. 21, No. 7.

GRAY W. A. (1986) 'Achieving employment equity and affirmative action through formalized mentoring'. Conference Proceedings of the National Conference On Management in the Public Sector, Victoria, BC, Canada, April 21–23.

HAMILTON R. (1993) *Mentoring*. London, the Industrial Society.

HAY J. (1993) 'A new approach to mentoring'. *Financial Training Review*. October.

HAY J. (1995) *Transformational Mentoring: Creating developmental alliances for changing organizational cultures*. Maidenhead, McGraw-Hill.

HAY J. (1997) *Action Mentoring: Creating your own developmental alliance*. Watford, Sherwood Publishing.

HAY J. (1998) 'Mentoring – traditional versus developmental'. *Organisations and People*. Vol. 5, No. 3, August.

HODGSON P. (1987) 'Managers can be taught but leaders have to learn'. *Industrial and Commercial Training*. November-December.

HOLLOWAY A. (1994) *Mentoring: The definitive workbook*. Manchester, Development Processes.

HUNT D. M. (1992) 'A longitudinal study of mentor outcomes'. *Mentoring International*. Vol. 6, No. 2–3, spring.

IBARRA H. (2000) 'Making partner: a mentor's guide to the psychological journey'. *Harvard Business Review*. Vol. 78, No. 2.

INDUSTRIAL RELATIONS SERVICES (1990a) 'Back to basics: mentoring'. Recruitment and development supplement to *Industrial Relations Review and Report*, 464, May.

INDUSTRIAL RELATIONS SERVICES (1990b) 'Mentors and their role in developing talent'. Recruitment and development supplement to *Industrial Relations Review and Report*, 462, April.

INDUSTRIAL SOCIETY (1995) *Managing Best Practice: Mentoring*. London, Industrial Society.

INDUSTRIAL SOCIETY *and* THE ITEM GROUP (1990) *The Line Manager's Role in Developing Talent*. London, Industrial Society.

KIZILOS P. (1990) 'Take my mentor, please'. *Training*. April.

KRAM K. (1980) 'Mentoring processes at work: developmental relationships in managerial careers'. Doctoral dissertation, Yale University.

KRAM K. (1983) 'Phases of the mentor relationship'. *Academy of Management Journal*. Vol. 26, No. 4.

KRAM K. (1985) 'Improving the mentoring process'. *Training and Development Journal*. April.

KRAM K. (1988) *Mentoring at Work*. Lanham, MD, University Press of America.

KRAM K. *and* ISABELLA L. A. (1983) 'Much ado about mentors, not enough about peers'. *Career Development Bulletin*.

KRAM K. *and* ISABELLA L. A. (1985) 'Mentoring alternatives: the role of peer relationships in career development'. *Academy of Management Journal*. March.

LEVINSON D. (1978) *The Seasons of a Man's Life*. New York, Alfred Knopf.

LEWIS G. (1993) *The Mentoring Manager*. London, Pitman.

LIKERT R. (1961) *New Patterns of Management*. New York, McGraw-Hill.

MACLENNAN N. (1995) *Coaching and Mentoring*. Aldershot, Gower.

MEGGINSON D. (1993) 'Three ways of mentoring'. *AMED/ Sundridge Park Conference Proceedings*.

MEGGINSON D. (1994a) 'Images of mentoring'. *EMC Research Conference*. Sheffield.

MEGGINSON D. (1994b) 'Planned and emergent learning: a framework and a method'. *Executive Development*. Vol. 7, No. 6.

MEGGINSON D. (2000) 'Current issues in mentoring'. *Career Development International*.

MEGGINSON D. *and* CLUTTERBUCK D. (1995) *Mentoring in Action: A practical guide for managers*. London, Kogan Page.

MUMFORD A. (1985) 'What's new in management development'. *Personnel Management*. May.

MURRAY M. *with* OWEN M. A. (1991) *Beyond the Myths and Magic of Mentoring*. San Francisco, Calif., Jossey-Bass.

NOE R. A. (1988) 'An investigation into the determinants of successful assigned mentoring relationships'. *Personnel Psychology*. Vol. 41.

NOLLER R. B. (1982) 'Mentoring: a renaissance of apprenticeship'. *Journal of Creative Behaviour*. Vol. 16.

O'NEILL R. M., HORTON S. *and* CROSBY F. J. (1999) 'Gender issues in developmental relationships', in A. J. Murrell, F. J. Crosby, R. J. Ely, and L. Erlbaum (eds), *Mentoring Dilemmas: Developmental relationships within multicultural organizations*. New Jersey, Lawrence Erlbaum Associates.

ORPEN C. (1997) 'The effects of formal mentoring on employee work motivation, organizational commitment and job performance'. *The Learning Organization*. Vol. 4, No. 2.

PARSLOE E. (1992) *Coaching, Mentoring and Assessing: A practical guide to developing competence*. London, Kogan Page.

PARSLOE E. (1999) 'A selection of letters'. *People Management*. 20 May.

RAGINS B. R. (1997a) 'Antecedents of diversified mentoring relationships'. *Journal of Vocational Behaviour.* Vol. 51.

RAGINS B. R. (1997b) 'Diversified mentoring relationships in organisations: a power perspective'. *Academy of Management Review.* Vol. 22, No. 2.

RAGINS B. R. *and* COTTON J. L. (1993) 'Gender and willingness to mentor in organisations'. *Academy of Management Journal.* Vol. 19, September.

RAGINS B. R. *and* COTTON J. L. (1996) 'Jumping the hurdles: the barriers to mentoring for women in organisations'. *Leadership and Organisation Development Journal.* Vol. 17, No. 3.

RAGINS B. R. *and* COTTON J. L. (1999) 'Mentor functions and outcomes: a comparison of men and women in formal and informal mentoring relationships'. *Journal of Applied Psychology.* Vol. 84, No. 4.

RAGINS B. R. *and* McFARLIN D. B. (1990) 'Perceptions of mentoring roles in cross-gender mentoring relationships'. *Journal of Vocational Behaviour.* Vol. 37.

RAGINS B. R. *and* SCANDURA T. A. (1993) 'The effects of sex and gender role orientation on mentorship in male dominated occupations'. *Journal of Vocational Behaviour.* Vol. 43.

RAGINS B. R. *and* SCANDURA T. A. (1994) 'Gender differences in expected outcomes of mentoring relationships'. *Academy of Management Journal.* Vol. 37, No. 4.

RAGINS B. R. *and* SCANDURA T. A. (1999) 'Burden or blessing? Expected costs and benefits of being a mentor'. *Journal of Organisational Behaviour.* Vol. 20.

REICH M. H. (1986) 'The mentor connection'. *Personnel.* February.

SCHRIESHEIM C. A. *and* MURPHY C. J. (1976) 'Relationships between leader behaviour and subordinate satisfaction and performance: a test of some situational moderators'. *Journal of Applied Psychology.* Vol. 61, No. 5. pp634–41.

SEGERMAN-PECK I. (1991) *Networking and Mentoring: A woman's guide*. London, Piatkus.

SMITH P. *and* WEST-BURNHAM J. (EDS) (1993) *Mentoring in the Effective Schools*. London, Longham.

STOTT A. *and* SWEENEY J. (1999) 'More than a match'. *People Management*. 30 June.

STRUTHERS N. J. (1995) 'Differences in mentoring: a function of gender or organizational rank?' *Journal of Social Behaviour and Personality*. Vol. 10.

THOMAS D. A. (1990) 'The impact of race on managers' experience of developmental relationships (mentoring and sponsorship): an intra-organizational study'. *Journal of Organisational Behaviour*. Vol. 11.

VIATOR R. E. (1999) 'An analysis of formal mentoring programs and perceived barriers to obtaining a mentor at large public accounting firms'. *Accounting Horizons*. Vol. 13, No. 1.

WALES S. (1998) 'Executive mentoring: a retrospective exploration of managers' experiences of external mentoring'. Dissertation for MSc in change agent skills and strategies, University of Surrey.

WILKIN M. (ED.) (1992) *Mentoring in Schools*. London, Kogan Page.

WRIGHT R. G. *and* WERTHER W. B. (1991) 'Mentors at work'. *Journal of Management Development*. Vol. 10, No. 3.

ZEY M. (1984) *The Mentor Connection*. New York, Dow Jones Irwin.

# INDEX